The Little Sarasota DINING Book.

2023

SARASOTA'S BEST SELLING RESTAURANT GUIDE

DINESARASOTA.COM

The Little Sarasota DINING Book.
14th Edition | 2023

To contact us, please send email to:
press@dinesarasota.com

Printed in the USA

10 9 8 7 6 5 4 3 2 1

ISBN 978-0-9862840-8-3

THANK YOU!

Thanks for picking up the 14th edition of our annual Sarasota dining book. We are so happy to be able to give you Sarasota restaurant information that you can use every day! But like most things in life, we couldn't do it without help.

Thanks to Andis Wines, Thai Branton, Bianca Colangelo, Christopher Covelli, John Dale, Myriam Dandonneau, Kelly Dungan, Tracy Freeman, Debbie Hoffman, Billy Hoyle, Lauren Jackson, Michael Klauber, Lorenzo Muslia, Joyce Norris, Martin Orozco-Ramirez, Joey Panek, and the Realm Restaurant Group for contributing content to this year's edition. It is fantastic to have such talented people in our community. And we're grateful for their help.

Cindi Kievit (print & digital) and Jen Hogan (digital) make sure it's actually possible for you to read all things we write about. Thank you for your editing skills and masterful use of the red pen.

As always, thanks to you! Thank you for supporting what we do. We're always striving to make sure that our local Sarasota restaurants get the attention they so richly deserve. I know that they appreciate you too!

Twenty years goes by basically in the blink of an eye. Why do I say that? Because that's how long dineSarasota has been doing its thing! YES, twenty years! It sure doesn't seem like it could possibly be true. But it is.

When we started this long, strange Sarasota restaurant trip in 2002, I had no idea we would still be going strong in 2023. Our brand is a lot stronger than it was back then. And it has expanded in so many different ways.

2023 marks the 14th annual edition of *The Little Sarasota DINING Book*. Our dineSarasota.com website now hosts hundreds of thousands of views per year. And our *Sarasota Bites* newsletter continues to pick up subscribers by the thousands. Who would have ever thought our little niche would be so popular? And it is ALL thanks to you!

We've got a bunch of great stuff planned for 2023. Yes, we'll be finishing up our year-long *A Burger A Week* series that comes in the newsletter. We've got a few upgrades to the website coming down the road. And, of course, we keep trying to make this best selling dining book just a little bit better every year.

We couldn't be happier that you've purchased our book. If you like it, we would love it if you would tell your friends about it. If you haven't subscribed to our newsletter, it would make us happy if you did (there are QR codes in this book to make that easy!).

We understand that making good dining decisions can sometimes be challenging. Our goal with all of this is to try and make those decisions just a bit easier. We're here to help!

Larry Hoffman
Publisher, dineSarasota.com

2023 DINESARASOTA TOP 50

- [ ] 1   GROVE Restaurant
- [ ] 2   Pier 22
- [ ] 3   Bijou Cafe Garden
- [ ] 4   Kore Steakhouse *
- [ ] 5   Mattison's Forty One
- [ ] 6   Drunken Poet
- [ ] 7   Michael's on East
- [ ] 8   Rosemary and Thyme
- [ ] 9   Meliora *
- [ ] 10   Café L'Europe
- [ ] 11   Fork & Hen *
- [ ] 12   Opus Restaurant & Lounge
- [ ] 13   Duval's Fresh. Local. Seafood.
- [ ] 14   Pho Cali
- [ ] 15   Summer House Steak & Seafood
- [ ] 16   Casey Key Fish House
- [ ] 17   Kiyoshi's Sushi
- [ ] 18   Turtles on Little Sarasota Bay
- [ ] 19   Island House Tap & Grill
- [ ] 20   Alpine Steak House
- [ ] 21   Munchies 420 Café
- [ ] 22   Old Salty Dog
- [ ] 23   Harry's Continental Kitchens
- [ ] 24   LobsterCraft *
- [ ] 25   St. Armands Oyster Bar *
- [ ] 26   Rosebud's Steakhouse & Seafood
- [ ] 27   Knick's Tavern & Grill
- [ ] 28   Phillippi Creek Oyster Bar
- [ ] 29   Stiks

❑	30	Libby's Neighborhood Bistro
❑	31	Yume Sushi
❑	32	Yoder's Restaurant
❑	33	Roessler's
❑	34	Little Saigon Bistro
❑	35	Flirt Sushi Lounge *
❑	36	1592 Wood Fired Kitchen
❑	37	Riverhouse Reef & Grill
❑	38	Athens Family Restaurant
❑	39	BLVD Cafe *
❑	40	Figaro Bistro
❑	41	Lobster Pot
❑	42	Brine Seafood & Raw Bar
❑	43	Star Thai & Sushi
❑	44	Ophelia's On The Bay
❑	45	Captain Curt's Crab & Oyster Bar
❑	46	Boca Kitchen, Bar, Market
❑	47	Good Liquid Brewing Company *
❑	48	Kacey's Seafood & More
❑	49	Apollonia Grill
❑	50	Screaming Goat Taqueria

Opened since our last edition.

HOW TO USE THIS CHECKLIST - Like you really need an explanation for this. But, just in case, here goes. Get out there and eat through our Top 50! We've made it easy for you to keep track of your culinary adventures. These are the restaurants that you've been searching for, clicking on, and downloading on our dineSarasota.com website all year. So in a way this is really *your* Top 50. And, if you flip to the back of this book, we've left a couple of note pages for you to keep track of your favorites. Go ahead, start your own Sarasota restaurant journal.

HOW TO USE THIS BOOK

Thanks for picking up a copy of the latest *Little Sarasota DINING Book*. We're hoping that you're going to use it as your go-to guide to Sarasota dining. Now that you're the proud owner of a copy, we're going to give you some helpful inside tips on how to use the guide.

First off, it's arranged alphabetically. So, if you know the alphabet, you can use our guide. Yes, it's really that easy. It has basic restaurant information in each listing. Name, address, phone... also lists the restaurant's website if you would like to go there for additional information.

In the outlined bar, it will tell you the neighborhood/area where the restaurant is located, the cuisine it serves, and its relative expense. It's relative to Sarasota, not NYC, keep that in mind.

We list the hours of operation for each restaurant. It helps to know when they are open. We try our best to make this info as accurate as possible. But sometimes, Sarasota restaurants have special seasonal hours. We apologize in advance if a place may have changed their hours after we went to print. If there's a question, it's always best to call the restaurant.

For each place we'll also tell you what you can expect. Is it noisy or quiet? Good for kids? Maybe a late night menu. It's not an exhaustive list, just some of the highlights to guide your dining decision-making process.

There aren't a lot of mysterious symbols that you have to reference. If you see this *, it means the restaurant has more than one location. We've listed what we consider to be the main one. The other locations are usually listed in the super handy cross reference in the back of the book.

Speaking of the cross reference, here's the scoop. Restaurants are listed in alphabetical order (you're good at that now!). We give you basic info. Name, address, phone. Restaurants are then listed by cuisine type and then by location. So, you can easily find that perfect seafood restaurant on Longboat Key.

QR CODES. Each restaurant listing has a little square box with a bunch of jumbled up dots. That's your easy access to the menu for that restaurant. Just scan that little code with the QR reader or camera on your smartphone and, just like magic, there's the menu! Pretty great, right? Oh, what if I don't have a smartphone? Well, then it just might be time...

OK. Here's where things really get interesting. You now know where things are located and what type of food you can expect. But, let's dive in a little deeper. Let's say you're just visiting beautiful, sunny Sarasota AND you've got kids. What would be a good choice? How about celebrating a special occasion or event? Or, maybe you would just like to eat a meal and enjoy a spectacular water view. Where's the best spot?

That's where our specialty categories come in. Here are some things to keep in mind. First, we've curated these restaurant lists just for you. Second, these places may not be the only ones in town that fit the description. But, we think they're among the best. Hey, why isn't my favorite pizza place on that list? We're not trying to snub anybody here, but there's only so much space.

LIVE MUSIC – Really self-explanatory. But, the music ranges from piano bar to acoustic guitar to rock 'n' roll. So, you may want to see who's playing the night you're going. Also, yes, there are other places in town that have live music.

CATERING – You could probably convince most restaurants to cater your twelve person dinner or throw together some to-go food for you to arrange on your own platters. The places listed here do it for REAL. They cater regularly.

EASY ON YOUR WALLET – A little perspective is in order here. Nothing on this list comes close to the McDonald's Dollar Menu (thankfully). That being said, these are some places you could go and not have to sell some jewelry to pay the tab. Something to keep in mind, "Easy on the wallet" depends a little on how big your billfold is. These restaurants won't break the budget.

NEW – No explanation necessary. These restaurants are "relatively" new. Some have been open longer than others. But, they've opened since our last edition.

SPORTS + FOOD + FUN – The big game is on and you want to see it. Here are some places that do that well. Lots of places have a TV in the bar. These go above and beyond that.

GREAT BURGERS – In the last half of 2022 and the first half of 2023, we are off on a Sarasota burger expedition. Our *A Burger A Week* series is running in our newsletter, *Sarasota Bites*. We'll give you some of the highlights in this burger listing.

NICE WINE LIST – Hmmm… A 2006 Cabernet or a 2015 Pouilly-Fuissé? That is one tough question. No "wine in a box" here. These restaurants all have a sturdy wine list and are proud of it. Sometimes it can certainly be a little intimidating choosing a wine. These spots usually have someone to hold your hand and walk you through it.

A BEAUTIFUL WATER VIEW – Nothing says Florida like a picture perfect view of the water. And, these places have that. The food runs the gamut from bar food to fine dining.

LATER NIGHT MENU – This is not New York, and it is not Miami or Chicago either. That is the context with which you should navigate this list. Notice we said "LATER" night menu and NOT "late night menu." We're a reasonably early dining town. The places listed here are open past the time when half of Sarasota is safely tucked in bed. They all might not be 1AM, but we do have a few choices if you're still out past 2am!

SARASOTA FINE DINING – It's not great when people look down their noses at our upscale dining scene. We have some damn good chefs here in Sarasota. And, they're showing off their skills every single day. They should be celebrated. This list may not contain Le Bernardin, Alinea, or The French Laundry. But, we have some REAL contenders.

Lastly, there is always the question, "How do these restaurants get into this book?" They are selected based on their yearly popularity on dineSarasota.com. These are the restaurants that YOU are interested in. You've been searching for them on our website all year long. There are no advertisements here. So, you can't "buy your way in." It's all you. This is really YOUR guide. And, I must say, you have great taste!

A SPRIG OF THYME
1962 Hillview Street
941-330-8890
asprigofthymesrq.com

SOUTHSIDE VILLAGE	EUROPEAN	COST: $$

HOURS: Tues-Sat, 5PM to 9PM
CLOSED SUNDAY & MONDAY (SUMMER ONLY)

WHAT TO EXPECT: Upscale, Casual • Good For A Date
European Bistro Feel • Good Wine List

BEST BITES: Buratta, Melon & Berry Salad • Canard Pyrenees
Snapper A 'La Basque • Poulet A ' La Francaise

SOME BASICS
Reservations:	YES
Spirits:	BEER/WINE
Parking:	STREET
Outdoor Dining:	YES

SCAN FOR MENU

ALMAZONICA CERVECERIA
4141 South Tamiami Trail
941-260-5964
almazonicacerveceria.com

SOUTH TRAIL	PERUVIAN	COST: $$

HOURS: Tues-Sat, 4PM to 10PM
CLOSED SUNDAY & MONDAY

WHAT TO EXPECT: Upscale • Small Batch Cerveceria (Brewery)
"Amazon Soul" • Lots Of Parking

BEST BITES: Ceviche! • Corazon Mio Anticucho
Arroz con Mariscos • Peruvian Churros • Pan Roasted Cod

SOME BASICS
Reservations:	YES
Spirits:	BEER/WINE
Parking:	LOT
Outdoor Dining:	NO

SCAN FOR MENU

ALPINE STEAKHOUSE & BUTHER SHOP
4520 South Tamiami Trail
941-922-3797
alpinesteak.com

SOUTH TRAIL	AMERICAN	COST: $$

HOURS: Tue to Sat, 9AM to 9PM
CLOSED SUNDAY & MONDAY

WHAT TO EXPECT: Great Butcher Shop • Home Of The "Turducken"
German Cuisine • Featured On The Food Network

BEST BITES: TurDuckHen • Steaks! • 1/2lb Sirloin Burger
German Sausage Sampler • Texas Baby Back Ribs

SCAN FOR MENU

SOME BASICS

Reservations:	NO
Spirits:	FULL BAR
Parking:	LOT
Outdoor Dining:	NO

AMA LA VITA RISTORANTE   `NEW`
1551 Main Street
941-960-1551
amalavitasrq.com

DOWNTOWN	ITALIAN	COST: $$$

HOURS: Wed-Sat, 5PM to 9PM
CLOSED SUNDAY, MONDAY & TUESDAY

WHAT TO EXPECT: Upscale Italian • Private Dining Available
Good Wine List • Downtown Location

BEST BITES: Artichoke Oreganata • Gnocchi Bolognese
Chicken Scarparello • Authentic Italian Desserts

SCAN FOR MENU

SOME BASICS

Reservations:	YES
Spirits:	BEER/WINE
Parking:	STREET
Outdoor Dining:	NO

AMORE RESTAURANT

180 North Lime Avenue
941-383-1111
amorelbk.com

	ITALIAN	COST: $$$

HOURS: Wed-Sun, 5PM to 9PM
CLOSED MONDAY & TUESDAY

WHAT TO EXPECT: Opentable Reservations • Upscale Italian Cuisine
Casual, Relaxed Atmosphere • Also A Portuguese Menu

BEST BITES: Pica-Pua de Vaca • Bacalhau Ribatenjo
Chicken Livornese • Salmon Picatta • Beef Osso Bucco

SOME BASICS

SCAN FOR MENU

Reservations: YES
Spirits: BEER/WINE
Parking: LOT
Outdoor Dining: NO

ANDREA'S

2085 Siesta Drive
941-951-9200
andreasrestaurantsrq.com

SOUTHGATE	ITALIAN	COST: $$$

HOURS: Mon-Sat, 5PM to 10PM
CLOSED SUNDAY (summer only)

WHAT TO EXPECT: Nice Wine List • Quiet Restaurant Atmosphere
Upscale Italian Cuisine • Great Special Occasion Place

BEST BITES: Polenta Concia • Tonnarelli Sunday Style
Veal Tripe Piemontese • Short Ribs Andreas

SOME BASICS

SCAN FOR MENU

Reservations: YES
Spirits: BEER/WINE
Parking: LOT
Outdoor Dining: NO

ANNA MARIA OYSTER BAR

6906 14th Street W.*
941-758-7880
oysterbar.net

BRADENTON	SEAFOOD	COST: $$

HOURS: Sun-Thur, 11AM to 9PM
Fri-Sat, 11AM to 10PM

WHAT TO EXPECT: Good For Kids • Casual, Family Atmosphere
Large Menu • Good For Groups

BEST BITES: Lots Of Raw Bar Options • Mussels Provencal
Conch Fritters • Pier Poke Bowl • Linguine With Scallops
Lobster Bisque • Gulf Grouper Sandwich • Live ME Lobster

SCAN FOR MENU

SOME BASICS

Reservations:	8 OR MORE
Spirits:	FULL BAR
Parking:	LOT
Outdoor Dining:	YES

ANNA'S DELI & SANDWICH SHOP

6535 Midnight Pass Road
941-349-4888
annasdelis.com

SIESTA KEY	DELI	COST: $

HOURS: Daily, 10:30AM to 4PM

WHAT TO EXPECT: Super Casual • Great Sandwiches (The Surfer)
Good For SK Beach To Go • Super Fast Service

BEST BITES: Sandwiches are what they do! • Surfer
Peddler • Villager • Skater • Fiesta

SCAN FOR MENU

SOME BASICS

Reservations:	NO
Spirits:	NONE
Parking:	LOT
Outdoor Dining:	NO

APOLLONIA GRILL

8235 Cooper Creek Boulevard*
941-359-4816
apolloniagrill.com

UPARK	GREEK	COST: $$

HOURS: Mon-Thur, 11:30AM to 9PM • Fri & Sat, 11:30AM to 10PM
Sunday, 11:30AM to 8:30PM

WHAT TO EXPECT: Good For Groups • Family Owned
Casual Dining • Lots Of Parking • Also A Landings Location

BEST BITES: Avegolemono Soup • Lamb Shank Osso Bucco
Seafood Salad • Spinach & Feta Flatbread • Moussaka

SOME BASICS

SCAN FOR MENU

Reservations:	YES
Spirits:	FULL BAR
Parking:	LOT
Outdoor Dining:	YES

ATHENS FAMILY RESTAURANT

2300 Bee Ridge Road
941-706-4121
athensfamilyrestaurant.business.site

	GREEK	COST: $$

HOURS: Mon-Sat, 8AM to 10PM
CLOSED SUNDAY

WHAT TO EXPECT: Casual Greek Cuisine • Good For Families
Family Owned & Operated • Lots Of Parking

BEST BITES: Greek Omelet • Bakaliaro Sandwich
Horiatiki Salad • Bifteki Platter • Baklava

SOME BASICS

SCAN FOR MENU

Reservations:	NO
Spirits:	BEER/WINE
Parking:	LOT
Outdoor Dining:	NO

ATMOSPHERE NEAPOLITAN PIZZERIA
935 North Beneva Road
941-203-8542

SARASOTA COMMONS	PIZZA	COST: $$

HOURS: Wed & Thur, 4PM to 9PM • Fri & Sat, 4PM to 10PM
Sun, 5PM to 9PM • CLOSED TUESDAY

WHAT TO EXPECT: Fantastic Neapolitan Pizza • Small, Cozy Setting
Italian Cuisine • Lots Of Parking

BEST BITES: Neapolitan Pizzas • Mortazza • Calzone
Sausage And Rapini • Calabria Spicy • Caserta

SCAN FOR INFO

SOME BASICS
Reservations:	YES
Spirits:	BEER/WINE
Parking:	LOT
Outdoor Dining:	NO

BABY BRIE'S CAFÉ & COFFEE HOUSE　　　NEW
1938 Adams Lane
941-362-0988

TOWLES COURT	AMERICAN	COST: $

HOURS: Mon-Fri, 9AM to 2:30PM • Sun, 8AM to 2PM
CLOSED SATURDAY

WHAT TO EXPECT: Great Outdoor Porch • Super Casual
Eclectic Towles Court Neighborhood

INSIDER TIP: Breakfast BLT • Avocado Toast • Breakfast Sammy
Turkey Bagel • LJ's Cubano Melt • Caprese Melt
Seasonal Soup Of The Day • Cranberry Apple Salad

SCAN FOR MENU

SOME BASICS
Reservations:	NONE
Spirits:	NONE
Parking:	LOT
Outdoor Dining:	YES

BAKER AND WIFE

2157 Siesta Drive
941-960-1765
bakerwife.com

SOUTHGATE	AMERICAN	COST: $$

HOURS: Thur-Sat, 5PM to 9PM

WHAT TO EXPECT: Artisan Pizza • Casual Atmosphere
Lots Of Dessert Choices • Opentable Reservations

BEST BITES: Beef Carpaccio • Spicy Tuna Tartare • Caesar Salad
Pan Seared Salmon • Buckhead Beef Grilled Skirt Steak
The Meatball • Pizza! • The Bakers Burger

SOME BASICS
Reservations: YES
Spirits: FULL BAR
Parking: LOT
Outdoor Dining: YES

SCAN FOR MENU

BAVARO'S PIZZA NAPOLETANA & PASTERIA

27 Fletcher Avenue
941-552-9131
bavarospizza.com

DOWNTOWN	PIZZA	COST: $$

HOURS: Sun-Thur, 5PM to 9PM
Fri & Sat, 5PM to 10PM

WHAT TO EXPECT: Casual Italian • Good For Families • Pizza!
Gluten Free Options • Opentable Reservations

BEST BITES: Pizza Napoletana • Italian Chopped Salad
Heirloom Bruschetta • Tagliatelle Bolognese • Tiramisu

SOME BASICS
Reservations: YES
Spirits: FULL BAR
Parking: LOT/STREET
Outdoor Dining: YES

SCAN FOR MENU

BEACH BISTRO

6600 Gulf Drive
941-778-6444
beachbistro.com

HOLMES BEACH	AMERICAN	COST: $$$$

HOURS: Daily, 5PM to 10PM

WHAT TO EXPECT: Fine Dining • Beautiful Gulf Views • Romantic
Perfect For A Special Occasion • Great Wine List & Cocktails

BEST BITES: Lobster & Shrimp Cocktail • LobsterCargots
Bistro Bouillabaisse • Maple Leaf Farms Duckling Breast

SCAN FOR MENU

SOME BASICS

Reservations:	YES
Spirits:	FULL BAR
Parking:	VALET
Outdoor Dining:	YES

BEACH HOUSE WATERFRONT RESTAURANT

200 Gulf Drive North
941-779-2222
beachhousedining.com

BRADENTON BEACH	AMERICAN	COST: $$

HOURS: Daily, 11:30AM to 10PM

WHAT TO EXPECT: Great For A Date • Florida Seafood
Nice Wine List • Lots Of Outdoor Dining Space

BEST BITES: House Smoked Fish-Dip • Gamble Farm House Salad
Seafood Gumbo • Short Rib Tacos • Key Lime Pie

SCAN FOR MENU

SOME BASICS

Reservations:	NO
Spirits:	FULL BAR
Parking:	LOT
Outdoor Dining:	YES

BEVARDI'S SALUTE! RESTAURANT

23 North Lemon Avenue
941-365-1020
salutesarasota.com

DOWNTOWN	ITALIAN	COST: $$

HOURS: Sun-Thur, 4PM to 10PM • Fri & Sat, 4PM to 11PM
Early Bird Dinner: Daily, 4pm to 6pm • CLOSED MONDAY

WHAT TO EXPECT: Live Music • In-House Catering
Opentable Reservations • Nice Outdoor Dining

BEST BITES: Salsiccia Salute • Caprese • Gnocchi Di Patate
Cotoletta Parmigiana • Branzino • Grilled Veal Chop

SOME BASICS

SCAN FOR MENU

Reservations:	YES
Spirits:	FULL BAR
Parking:	STREET/LOT
Outdoor Dining:	YES

BIG WATER FISH MARKET

6641 Midnight Pass Road
941-554-8101
bigwaterfishmarket.com

SIESTA KEY	SEAFOOD	COST: $$

HOURS: Mon-Sat, 11AM to 9PM
Sunday, 12PM to 8PM

WHAT TO EXPECT: Fresh Fish Market • Casual Dining
SK South Bridge Location • Key Lime Pie!

BEST BITES: Conch Cakes • "Jacks" Fish Stew • Hogfish
Grouper Reuben • Stone Crab (in season) • Key Lime Pie

SOME BASICS

SCAN FOR MENU

Reservations:	NO
Spirits:	BEER/WINE
Parking:	LOT
Outdoor Dining:	NO

BIJOU GARDEN CAFÉ
1287 First Street
941-366-8111
bijoucafe.net

DOWNTOWN	AMERICAN	COST: $$$

HOURS: Tue-Thur, 5PM to 9PM • Fri & Sat, 5PM to 10PM
CLOSED SUNDAY & MONDAY

WHAT TO EXPECT: Great For A Date • Excellent Wine List
Opentable Reservations • Private Dining Program

BEST BITES: Truffle Butternut Squash Soup • Escargot Bourguignon
Open Faced Lobster Ravioli • Roasted Half Peking Duck
Pommes Gratin Dauphinois • Maple Bread Pudding

SCAN FOR MENU

SOME BASICS

Reservations:	YES
Spirits:	FULL BAR
Parking:	VALET
Outdoor Dining:	YES

BLU KOUZINA
25 North Boulevard of Presidents
941-388-2619
blukouzina.com/US

ST. ARMANDS	GREEK	COST: $$$

HOURS: Daily, 11:30AM to 8:30PM

WHAT TO EXPECT: Nice Wine List • Real Greek Cuisine
Opentable Reservations • Many Small Plate Appetizers

BEST BITES: Taramosalata • Dolmades • Keftedes
Kalamaki Souvlaki • Roast Lemon Chicken
Lamb Kabob • Mousaka • Octopus • Pastitsio

SCAN FOR MENU

SOME BASICS

Reservations:	YES
Spirits:	BEER/WINE
Parking:	STREET
Outdoor Dining:	YES

BLUE KOI

`NEW`

3801 McIntosh Road
941-388-7738
bluekoisushi.com

	SUSHI	COST: $$

HOURS: LUNCH: Wed-Fri, 11:30AM to 1:30PM • CLOSED SUNDAY
DINNER: Mon-Thur, 5PM to 9PM • Fri & Sat, 4PM to 9PM

WHAT TO EXPECT: Carryout & Delivery Only • Super Creative Sushi
Catering Available • Online Ordering

INSIDER TIP: Sushi Combo • Family Platter • Poke Bowls
Seared Ahi Tuna Salad • Salmon Bowl • Miso Soup

SCAN FOR MENU

SOME BASICS

Reservations:	NONE
Spirits:	NONE
Parking:	LOT
Outdoor Dining:	NO

BLVD CAFE

`NEW`

1580 Boulevard of the Arts
941-203-8102
blvdcafesrq.com

ROSEMARY DIST.	AMERICAN	COST: $$

HOURS: Wed-Mon, 7AM to 5PM
CLOSED TUESDAY

WHAT TO EXPECT: Super Casual • Breakfast & Lunch Only
Lots Of Parking • Great Sidewalk Seating

INSIDER TIP: Burrata Frittata • Spring Pea and Leek Soup
Pate De Campagne Forestier • Seared Salmon Salad
Croque Monsieur • Open Faced Brooklyn Bagel

SCAN FOR MENU

SOME BASICS

Reservations:	NONE
Spirits:	NONE
Parking:	STREET
Outdoor Dining:	YES

Transition Sarasota
Behind Our Local "Gleaning" Organization
By Joyce Norris, Executive Director

Transition Sarasota is a non-profit organization committed to developing community-driven solutions for our local food system. Volunteers with their Suncoast Gleaning Project harvest excess produce from local farms to feed those who are food insecure.

Not only does gleaning provide food for those in need, but it also contributes to solving the environmental problem of food waste. The project is a great way to educate the community on these important issues and gives volunteers the opportunity to help their community. By harvesting produce otherwise left in fields, Suncoast Gleaning Project volunteers have the opportunity to take home some fresh food, as well as to donate to local food banks that are typically oversaturated with packaged foods. Volunteer gleaners often see a truck from The Food Bank of Manatee or All Faiths Food Bank drive onto the farm to collect the fresh produce they just harvested!

Transition Sarasota was founded in 2010 and, since then, has donated over 480,000 pounds of fresh produce to local food banks and pantries. During an entire farm glean in May 2022, volunteer gleaners stepped up to rescue 39,000 pounds of produce in only four days! Generous farm partners include Enza Zaden, Brown's Grove, Albritton Fruit Farms, and 4 Star Tomato. Transition Sarasota is always looking for more farm partners interested in food rescue. If you are a farmer and would like to find out more about gleaning and how you can help our community, please contact Exec@TransitionSRQ.org.

As an expansion of The Suncoast Gleaning Project, Suncoast Fruit Rescue was created as a means to collect excess or unharvested local fruit from backyard and neighborhood trees to donate to area food banks and charitable groups. The program really took off in 2021, with 1,600 pounds of backyard fruit rescued so far. You can register your tree at *transitionsrq. org/fruitrescue*. Suncoast Fruit Rescue volunteers will harvest and donate your excess, unwanted fruit to a local food bank or charity. This gets food to people in our community who need it and helps keep your yard clean!

Each year in October, Transition Sarasota hosts Eat Local Week. This is a week of engaging educational events celebrating food and farming in Sarasota and Manatee Counties. Partners come together to offer events, including garden tours, workshops, cooking demos, and hands-on activities. Eat Local Week exists to spark dialogue, build community, and showcase our local food system. Eating local and supporting local businesses helps to build community resilience and ensures that our community thrives.

Transition Sarasota also offers an online Eat Local Guide on its website. This is a great resource for locally sourced food, such as farmers' markets and farm stands, Community Supported Agriculture boxes, grow-your-own supplies, and restaurants serving locally sourced food. Looking for area farmers' markets or a restaurant serving local food? Here's your resource!

Throughout the year, Transition Sarasota offers fun, educational experiences to build community and provide valuable guidance and practical skills to attendees. Events have included edible garden tours, local honey tastings, workshops, and lectures.

To learn more about Transition Sarasota, please visit their website at *transitionsrq.org*. There are many ways to get involved, including volunteering for gleaning or becoming a member.

Transition Sarasota is a non-profit organization committed to developing community-driven solutions for our local food system. Volunteers with their Suncoast Gleaning Project harvest excess produce from local farms to donate to local food banks to feed those who are food insecure. Gleaning (harvesting for charity) not only provides food for those in need, it also contributes to solving the environmental problem of food waste.

BOCA SARASOTA

19 South Lemon Avenue
941-256-3565
bocasarasota.com

DOWNTOWN	AMERICAN	COST: $$

HOURS: Mon-Fri, 11AM to 10PM • Sat, 10AM to 11PM
Sun, 10AM to 10PM

WHAT TO EXPECT: Sat & Sun Brunch • Online Reservations
Classic Cocktails • Craft Beer Selections

BEST BITES: Skirt Steak • 60 Spiced Chicken • OMG Burger
Smoked Fish Dip • Flatbreads! • Kale Caesar
Chopped Salad • Guava Cheesecake & Plant City

SCAN FOR MENU

SOME BASICS

Reservations:	YES
Spirits:	FULL BAR
Parking:	STREET
Outdoor Dining:	YES

BOHEMIOS WINE & BEER TAPAS BAR

3246 Clark Road
941-260-9784
srqbohemios.com

	TAPAS	COST: $$

HOURS: Mon-Thur, 4PM to 10PM • Fri & Sat, 4PM to 12AM
CLOSED SUNDAY

WHAT TO EXPECT: Good Sized Wine List • Great Small Plate Dishes
Intimate Dining Atmosphere • Lots Of Parking

BEST BITES: Caprese Bruschetta • Chistorra • Gamba Scampi
Shrimp & Chorizo Stew • Lamb Lollipops • Ahi Tuna
Bohemios Churrasco • Tres Leches • Lava Cake

SCAN FOR MENU

SOME BASICS

Reservations:	YES
Spirits:	BEER/WINE
Parking:	LOT
Outdoor Dining:	NO

BONJOUR FRENCH CAFÉ

5214 Ocean Boulevard
941-346-0600
bonjourfrenchcafe.com

SIESTA KEY	FRENCH	COST: $$

HOURS: Daily, 7:30AM to 2:30PM

WHAT TO EXPECT: Super Casual • Great Outdoor Dining
Great Crepes!

BEST BITES: Eggs Benedict • Crepes • Belgian Waffles
Omelet "La Parisienne" • Croissants • Quiche Lorraine
Baguette Sandwiches • Nicoise Salad • Sea Ocean Salad

SOME BASICS

SCAN FOR MENU

Reservations:	NONE
Spirits:	BEER/WINE
Parking:	STREET
Outdoor Dining:	YES

THE BREAKFAST COMPANY

NEW

7246 55th Avenue E.
941-201-6002
thebreakfastcompanyfl.com

BRADENTON	AMERICAN	COST: $$

HOURS: Tues-Sun, 7AM to 2PM
CLOSED MONDAY

WHAT TO EXPECT: Breakfast & Lunch Only • Local Ingredients
Good For Families • Opening 2023 In The Landings

BEST BITES: Large Omelet Selection • Skillet Bowls
Terri's Famous Quiche • Strawberry Nutella French Toast
Scratch-Made Soups • California Cobb Salad

SOME BASICS

SCAN FOR MENU

Reservations:	NO
Spirits:	NONE
Parking:	LOT
Outdoor Dining:	YES

THE BREAKFAST HOUSE

1817 Fruitville Road
941-366-6860

DOWNTOWN	AMERICAN	COST: $$

HOURS: Wed-Sun, 8AM to 2PM
CLOSED MONDAY & TUESDAY

WHAT TO EXPECT: Charming Atmosphere • Breakfast & Lunch
Great Omelets • Eclectic

BEST BITES: Lots Of Omelet Selections • Belgian Waffles
Lavender Stuffed Blueberry Pancakes • Vegan Skillet

SCAN FOR INFO

SOME BASICS

Reservations:	NO
Spirits:	NONE
Parking:	LOT
Outdoor Dining:	YES

BREWBURGERS PUB & GRILL

370 Commercial Court
941-484-2337
brewburgers.com

VENICE	AMERICAN	COST: $$

HOURS: Daily, 11AM to 10PM

WHAT TO EXPECT: Super Casual • Try Brewburgers Back Porch!
"Icy Cold" Craft Beer Selection • Growler Fill Station

BEST BITES: Homemade "Saratoga" Chips • Lots of Burgers!!
Brew House Salad • Cheeseburger Club • Chili Fries
Tammy's Tot Basket • Brewburgers Cuban

SCAN FOR MENU

SOME BASICS

Reservations:	NONE
Spirits:	BEER/WINE
Parking:	LOT
Outdoor Dining:	NO

BRICK'S SMOKED MEATS
1528 State Street
941-993-1435
brickssmokedmeats.com

DOWNTOWN	BBQ	COST: $$

HOURS: Sun-Thur, 11AM to 10PM • Friday, 11AM to 11PM
Saturday, 10AM to 1PM

WHAT TO EXPECT: State Street Garage • Bbq, Bbq, Bbq
Good Local Beer List • Upbeat Atmosphere • Catering

BEST BITES: Pulled Pork • USDA Prime Brisket • St. Louis Ribs
Chicken Fried Chicken • Smoked Wings • Brisket Chili
Bacon Burnt Ends Tacos • State Street Corn

SOME BASICS
SCAN FOR MENU

Reservations:	NONE
Spirits:	FULL BAR
Parking:	STREET/GARAGE
Outdoor Dining:	YES

BRINE SEAFOOD & RAW BAR
2250 Gulf Gate Drive
941-404-5639
BrineSarasota.com

GULF GATE	SEAFOOD	COST: $$

HOURS: Sun-Thur, 11AM to 10PM
Fri & Sat, 11AM to 11PM

WHAT TO EXPECT: Raw Bar • Northeastern Style Seafood
Busy During Season • Vibrant Atmosphere

BEST BITES: Oysters on the Half Shell • Charred Octopus
Cream of Crab Soup • Jumbo Lump Crab Cakes
Pan Seared Snapper • Lobster Roll • Crab Cake Sandwich

SOME BASICS
SCAN FOR MENU

Reservations:	YES
Spirits:	FULL BAR
Parking:	LOT/STREET
Outdoor Dining:	YES

BROOKLYN BAGELS & DELI

6970 South Beneva Road*
941-993-1577
brooklynbagelsanddeli.com

DELI	COST: $$

HOURS: Daily, 7AM to 2PM

WHAT TO EXPECT: NY Style Bagels • Small Dining In Area
Friendly Service • Lots Of Parking

BEST BITES: Taylor Ham, Egg & Cheese Bagel • 20+ Bagel Flavors!
Kielbasa, Egg & Cheese • Pressed Cuban Sandwich
NY Club • Corned Beef & Hot Pastrami Sandwich

SCAN FOR MENU

SOME BASICS

Reservations:	NO
Spirits:	NONE
Parking:	LOT
Outdoor Dining:	YES

BUTTERMILK HANDCRAFTED FOOD

5520 Palmer Boulevard
941-487-8949

SOUTH TRAIL	ITALIAN	COST: $$

HOURS: Tues-Fri, 7AM to 1PM • Sat, 8AM to 1PM
CLOSED SUNDAY & MONDAY

WHAT TO EXPECT: Great Homemade Baked Goods • Small Menu
Counter Service Only

BEST BITES: Specialty Coffee • Homemade Cookies
Biscuit Sandwiches • Avocado Toast • Espresso

SCAN FOR INFO

SOME BASICS

Reservations:	NO
Spirits:	NONE
Parking:	LOT
Outdoor Dining:	YES

CAFÉ BARBOSSO

5501 Palmer Crossing Circle
941-922-7999
cafebarbosso.com

PALMER CROSSING	ITALIAN	COST: $$

HOURS: Tues-Sun, 4PM to 9PM
CLOSED MONDAY

WHAT TO EXPECT: Authentic NYC Italian • Casual Dining
Fun Dining Experience • Good For Groups

BEST BITES: Mozzarella in Carrozza • Fresh Mozzarella Caprese
Grandma's Spaghettini 'n Meatballs • Seafood Fra Diavolo
Chicken Marsala or Piccata • Personal Pizzas!

SOME BASICS

SCAN FOR MENU

Reservations:	YES
Spirits:	FULL BAR
Parking:	LOT
Outdoor Dining:	YES

CAFÉ EPICURE

1298 North Palm Avenue
941-366-5648
cafeepicure.com

DOWNTOWN	ITALIAN	COST: $$

HOURS: Daily, 11:45AM to 10:30PM

WHAT TO EXPECT: Great For A Date • Wood Fired Pizza
Casual Italian Fare • Palm Avenue Garage

BEST BITES: Salumeria - Formaggi & Salumi • Tartare Di Tonni
Pappardelle Bolognese • Pasta E Fagioli
Milanese Di Pollo • Pizza • Filetto Di Salmone

SOME BASICS

SCAN FOR MENU

Reservations:	YES
Spirits:	FULL BAR
Parking:	STREET/PALM GARAGE
Outdoor Dining:	YES

CAFÉ GABBIANO

5104 Ocean Boulevard
941-349-1423
cafegabbiano.com

SIESTA KEY	ITALIAN	COST: $$$

HOURS: Daily, 5PM to 10PM

WHAT TO EXPECT: Great Wine List • Siesta Village Location
Lots Of Parking • Opentable Reservations • Nightly Specials

BEST BITES: Formaggi & Salumi Plate • Bruschetta di Ischia
The Poached Pear • Costolette di Vitello • Ossobuco Ravioli
Branzino • Lasagne Bolognese

SCAN FOR MENU

SOME BASICS

Reservations:	YES
Spirits:	FULL BAR
Parking:	LOT
Outdoor Dining:	YES

CAFÉ L'EUROPE

431 St. Armands Circle
941-388-4415
cafeleurope.net

ST. ARMANDS	EUROPEAN	COST: $$$

HOURS: Tues-Sun, 11AM to 9PM
CLOSED MONDAY

WHAT TO EXPECT: Weekend Brunch • Special Wine Dinners
Fine Dining Since 1973 • Opentable Reservations

BEST BITES: Escargot • Oysters Rockefeller • French Onion Gratinee
Wedge Salad • Australian Rack of Lamb • French Grouper
Osso Bucco • Veal Piccata

SCAN FOR MENU

SOME BASICS

Reservations:	YES
Spirits:	FULL BAR
Parking:	VALET/STREET
Outdoor Dining:	YES

CAFE VENICE

101 W Venice Avenue
941-484-1855
cafevenicerestaurantandbar.com

VENICE	ECLECTIC	COST: $$$

HOURS: Tues-Sat, 11:30AM to 9PM
CLOSED SUNDAY & MONDAY

WHAT TO EXPECT: Super Eclectic Menu • LIVE Music
Catering Available • Downtown Venice Location

BEST BITES: Seared Scallops • Café Venice Mussels • Venice Caesar
Venice Caprese • Bouillabaisse • Crispy Roasted Duck
Pork Osso Bucco • Famous Crispy Spinach

SOME BASICS

SCAN FOR MENU

Reservations:	YES
Spirits:	FULL BAR
Parking:	STREET
Outdoor Dining:	YES

CAPTAIN CURT'S CRAB & OYSTER BAR

1200 Old Stickney Point Road
941-349-3885
captaincurts.com

SIESTA KEY	SEAFOOD	COST: $$

HOURS: Daily, 11AM to 2AM

WHAT TO EXPECT: Good For Kids • Super Casual • Lots Of Seafood
Ohio State Football HQ • Live Music • "Sniki Tiki"

BEST BITES: Award Winning Clam Chowder • Grouper Sandwich
Snow Crab Platter • Buffalo Wings! • Stone Crab (in season)
Alaskan Fish and Chips • Crab Cake Sandwich

SOME BASICS

SCAN FOR MENU

Reservations:	NO
Spirits:	FULL BAR
Parking:	LOT
Outdoor Dining:	YES

CARAGIULOS

69 South Palm Avenue
941-951-0866
caragiulos.com

DOWNTOWN	ITALIAN	COST: $$

HOURS: Sun-Thur, 4:30PM to 9:30PM
Fri & Sat, 4:30PM to 10:30PM

WHAT TO EXPECT: Casual Dining • Palm Ave. Gallery District
Good For Kids • Good For Groups

BEST BITES: Roman Artichokes • Salumi e Formaggi Board
Roasted Beet & Avocado Salad • Chopped 1989 Salad
Picatta Style Veal • Pizza! • Local Grouper

SCAN FOR MENU

SOME BASICS

Reservations:	YES
Spirits:	FULL BAR
Parking:	STREET/VALET
Outdoor Dining:	YES

CASEY KEY FISH HOUSE

801 Blackburn Point Road
941-966-1901
caseykeyfishhouse.com

OSPREY	SEAFOOD	COST: $$

HOURS: Daily, 11:30AM to 9PM

WHAT TO EXPECT: Vacation Atmosphere • Local Seafood
Boat Docks • Old Florida Feel • Live Music

BEST BITES: U Peel U Eat Shrimp • New England Clam Chowder
Grouper Sandwich • Shrimp Scampi • Seafood Pasta
Diver Scallops with Citrus Sauce • Key Lime Pie

SCAN FOR MENU

SOME BASICS

Reservations:	NO
Spirits:	FULL BAR
Parking:	LOT
Outdoor Dining:	YES

C'EST LA VIE!
1553 Main Street
941-906-9575
cestlaviesarasota.com

DOWNTOWN	FRENCH	COST: $$

HOURS: Mon-Wed, 7:30AM to 6PM • Thur-Sat, 7:30AM to 10PM
Sunday, 8:30AM to 5PM

WHAT TO EXPECT: Outdoor Tables • Relaxed Cafe Dining
Fantastic Bakery • Opentable Reservations

BEST BITES: Le Petit Déjeuner • Chocolate Croissant • Crepes
Baguette Sandwiches • Omelets • Quiche Lorraine
Croq' Madame • Parisienne Salad

SOME BASICS

SCAN FOR MENU

Reservations:	YES
Spirits:	BEER/WINE
Parking:	STREET
Outdoor Dining:	YES

CHA CHA COCONUTS TROPICAL BAR
417 St. Armands Circle
941-388-3300
chacha-coconuts.com

ST. ARMANDS	AMERICAN	COST: $$

HOURS: Sun-Thur, 11AM to 10PM
Fri & Sat, 11AM to 11PM

WHAT TO EXPECT: Good For Kids • Lot Of Outdoor Tables
Bustling Atmosphere • LIVE Music

BEST BITES: Grouper Bites • Calypso Chicken Wings
Peel & Eat Shrimp • Tony Salad • Grouper Tacos
Cuban Mixed Sandwich • Divi Divi Burger • Key Lime Pie

SOME BASICS

SCAN FOR MENU

Reservations:	NO
Spirits:	FULL BAR
Parking:	STREET/GARAGE/VALET
Outdoor Dining:	YES

Where to Find Social Media-Worthy Snacks In SRQ

Lauren Jackson

Snap it, post it, swipe it, and like it. In an ever-evolving digital world, food remains at the forefront of social media. With millions of content creators on Instagram and TikTok, it can seem impossible to stay on top of food trends. Which begs the question, where can you get a social media-worthy snack in Sarasota?

For diners, a decadent meal can rack up the likes, with images of food you would never dream of making at home. It doesn't have to be of the three Michelin star ilk, and won't be here in town, for the folks at Michelin have not discovered us—yet.

For something more accessible, try a heaping sandwich filled with your favorite deli meat and crowned with crisp vegetables. The bigger the bite, the better the views. At Faicco's on Webber, the sandwiches are almost too pretty to eat, and at Main Bar Sandwich Shop, the history makes for as good of a caption as the photo itself.

Décor also makes for an excellent photo. More restaurants are installing greenery walls, with neon signs screaming catchy phrases like "Don't Kill My Vibes," which you can find at Mochinut on University Parkway. Owner Lee Chu has crafted her doughnut and boba tea shop for the Gen Z gaze, complete with a stationary Vespa for content curators to straddle while eating their decorated pastries.

In Sarasota, there is no shortage of like-worthy scenery. Sprawling bayfront views, blue skies and enviable weather make outdoor captures a dime a dozen. But throw in a deep-fried hotdog, like the one at Old Salty Dog City Island, and you've got the perfect post. Ocean views, and over-the-top indulgence are sure to generate heart emojis from your jealous friends.

Over at Fork and Hen, they've tapped into a viral trend that will never die, fried chicken. Crisp deep-fried chicken comes served on a bun, on a platter, or even on a waffle with honey lavender butter. The only difficulty you will face is holding back the first bite before snapping a quick shot for social. And the likes keep pouring in.

And don't forget about ice cream, a Sarasota staple. Shooting a double-scoop waffle cone at Kilwin's on St. Armands Circle is a long-time tradition, although you'll never be able to finish it before it melts on a hot Florida day. Or, for an icy treat that no one in your friends list has ever seen before, try out Vampire Penguin. They call it snow, and top it with anything you can imagine, like lychee jelly or mango boba.

On your social media journey through town, don't forget the seafood. A seafood tower a lá Veronica Fish & Oyster is the ultimate decadence. But for something more down-home, it's the grouper sandwich that reigns supreme over Southwest Florida. Head over to the tiki thatched roof at Walt's Fish Market for an iconic sandwich in an iconic restaurant, check and check.

Whatever your social media goals, whether to share with friends or become the next influencer, Sarasota is teeming with spots to keep your followers entertained. As the leader of your own journey, you only have to decide where to try next.

Lauren Jackson is the Eat & Drink Editor for Sarasota Magazine. As a Sarasota native, she knows where to find the hidden gems in town. Although she isn't great at keeping a secret, she is good at finding the next hot spot.

CHATEAU 13

535 13th Street W.
941-226-0110
chateau-13.com

BRADENTON	EUROPEAN	COST: $$$

HOURS: Tues-Sat, 5PM to CLOSE
CLOSED SUNDAY & MONDAY

WHAT TO EXPECT: • Great Wine List • Great For A Special Occasion
Upscale Dining Experience • "Château To Go"

BEST BITES: Seared Foie Gras • Beef Tartare • Mussels Vin Blanc
Roquefort and Pear Salad • Basque Seafood Stew
Duck Leg Confit • Mousse au Chocolat

SCAN FOR MENU

SOME BASICS

Reservations:	YES
Spirits:	BEER/WINE
Parking:	STREET
Outdoor Dining:	NO

CIRCO

1435 2nd Street
941-253-0978
circosrq.com

DOWNTOWN	MEXICAN	COST: $$

HOURS: Mon, 4PM to 10PM • Tue, 11AM to 10PM • Sun, 12PM to 9PM
Wed-Thur, 12PM to 10PM • Fri & Sat, 12PM to 11PM

WHAT TO EXPECT: Super Casual • "Taco & Bourbon Joint"
Good For A Group • Catering Available

BEST BITES: Chips & Elote Corn Salsa • Tijuana Salad
Tamale Cake • Picnic Chicken Tacos • Walking Taco
Mongolian Beef Taco • Ahi Poke Taco

SCAN FOR MENU

SOME BASICS

Reservations:	NO
Spirits:	FULL BAR
Parking:	STREET/GARAGE
Outdoor Dining:	YES

CLASICO ITALIAN CHOPHOUSE
1341 Main Street
941-957-0700
clasicosrq.com

DOWNTOWN	ITALIAN	COST: $$

HOURS: Mon & Tue, 11:30AM to 11PM • Wed-Fri, 11:30AM to 12AM
Sat, 10AM to 12AM • Sun, 10AM to 11AM

WHAT TO EXPECT: Great For A Date • Live Music • Energetic Scene
Sat. & Sun. Brunch • Happy Hour Specials

BEST BITES: Tomato Bruschetta • Beef Carpaccio • Raw Bar
Gorgonzola Steak Gnocchi • Braised Short Rib
Italian Chopped Salad • Pizza!

SOME BASICS
SCAN FOR MENU

Reservations:	YES
Spirits:	FULL BAR
Parking:	STREET/PALM GARAGE
Outdoor Dining:	YES

CLAYTON'S SIESTA GRILLE
1256 Old Stickney Point Road
941-349-2800
claytonssiestagrille.com

SIESTA KEY	AMERICAN	COST: $$$

HOURS: Sun-Thur, 4PM to 10PM
Fri & Sat, 4PM to 10:30PM

WHAT TO EXPECT: Siesta Key Casual • Good For Groups
Convenient To SK South Bridge

BEST BITES: PEI Mussels • House Meatballs •
Siesta Seafood Chowder • Trout Almondine
Porcini Dusted Chicken • Brick Oven Pizza

SOME BASICS
SCAN FOR MENU

Reservations:	YES
Spirits:	FULL BAR
Parking:	STREET/PALM GARAGE
Outdoor Dining:	YES

THE COLUMBIA RESTAURANT
411 St. Armands Circle
941-388-3987
columbiarestaurant.com

ST. ARMANDS	CUBAN/SPANISH	COST: $$$

HOURS: Sun-Thur, 11AM to 9PM
Fri & Sat, 11AM to 10PM

WHAT TO EXPECT: Fantastic Sangria • Excellent Service
Opentable Reservations • Very Busy In Season

BEST BITES: 1905 Salad • Cuban Black Bean Soup • Cuban Sandwich
Empanadas de Picadillo • Roast Pork "a la Cubana"
Snapper a la Rusa • Flan

SCAN FOR MENU

SOME BASICS
Reservations:	YES
Spirits:	FULL BAR
Parking:	STREET/GARAGE
Outdoor Dining:	YES

CONNOR'S STEAKHOUSE
3501 South Tamiami Trail
941-260-3232
connorsrestaurant.com

SOUTHGATE	STEAKHOUSE	COST: $$$

HOURS: Sun-Thur, 11AM to 10PM
Fri & Sat, 11AM to 11PM

WHAT TO EXPECT: Lots Of Parking • Large Menu
Lots Of Wines By The Glass • Opentable Reservations

BEST BITES: Jumbo Shrimp Cocktail • Truffled Deviled Eggs
Lobster Crab Bisque • Espresso Rub Ribeye
Chilean Sea Bass Oscar • Chicken Piccata

SCAN FOR MENU

SOME BASICS
Reservations:	YES
Spirits:	FULL BAR
Parking:	LOT/VALET
Outdoor Dining:	YES

THE COTTAGE
153 Avenida Messina
941-312-9300
cottagesiestakey.com

SIESTA KEY	AMERICAN	COST: $$

HOURS: Sun-Thur, 11AM to 10PM
Fri & Sat, 11AM to 11PM

WHAT TO EXPECT: Tapas • Siesta Village • Outdoor Dining
Vacation Atmosphere • Nice Craft Beer Selection

BEST BITES: Grouper Sandwich • Billionaire Burger
Lobster Bisque • Tuna Tacoshimi • Black Mussels
Beef Short Ribs Sofrito • Siesta Seafood Scampi

SOME BASICS
SCAN FOR MENU

Reservations:	NO
Spirits:	FULL BAR
Parking:	STREET/VALET
Outdoor Dining:	YES

CRAB & FIN
420 St. Armands Circle
941-388-3964
crabfinrestaurant.com

ST. ARMANDS	SEAFOOD	COST: $$$

HOURS: Sun-Thur, 11:30AM to 9PM
Fri & Sat, 11:30AM to 9:30PM

WHAT TO EXPECT: Great For A Date • Sunday Brunch
Online Reservations • Early Dining Options

BEST BITES: Norwegian Sea Opilio Snow Crab • Raw Bar
Whole Local Mangrove Snapper • Alaskan Halibut
Gazpacho • Prime Butcher's Block Pork Ribeye

SOME BASICS
SCAN FOR MENU

Reservations:	YES
Spirits:	FULL BAR
Parking:	STREET/LOT
Outdoor Dining:	YES

THE CROW'S NEST

1968 Tarpon Center Drive
941-484-9551
crowsnest-venice.com

VENICE	SEAFOOD	COST: $$

HOURS: Lunch: Daily, 11:30AM to 3PM
Sun-Thur, 4:30PM to 9PM • Fri & Sat, 4:30PM to 9:30PM

WHAT TO EXPECT: Water View • Good Wine List
Opentable Reservations

BEST BITES: Raw Bar • Classic Shrimp Cocktail • Seafood Tower
Seafood Bisque • Oysters Rockefeller • Escargots
Bouillabaisse • 12oz Ribeye • Chicken Piccata

SCAN FOR MENU

SOME BASICS

Reservations:	YES
Spirits:	FULL BAR
Parking:	LOT
Outdoor Dining:	YES

CURRY STATION

3550 Clark Road
941-924-7222
currystation.net

	INDIAN	COST: $$

HOURS: Lunch Buffet: Mon-Sat, 11:30AM to 2:30PM
Dinner: Mon-Sat, 5PM to 9:30PM • CLOSED SUNDAY

WHAT TO EXPECT: Huge Indian Menu • Lots Of Curries
A Dozen Naan And Other Breads • Online Reservations

BEST BITES: Veg Samosa • Aloo Tikki Chat • Tandoor Chicken Tikka
Butter Chicken • Chicken Korma • Shrimp Biryani
Lamb Vindaloo • Seafood Curry • Chana Masala

SCAN FOR MENU

SOME BASICS

Reservations:	YES
Spirits:	BEER/WINE
Parking:	LOT
Outdoor Dining:	NO

DAIQUIRI DECK RAW BAR

5250 Ocean Boulevard*
941-349-8697
daiquirideck.com

SIESTA KEY	AMERICAN	COST: $$

HOURS: Sun-Thur, 11AM to 11PM
Fri & Sat, 11AM to 1AM

WHAT TO EXPECT: Great After Beach Stop • Super Casual
Good For Families • Dozens Of Frozen Daiquiri Flavors!

BEST BITES: Lots Of Oysters • Siesta Fiesta Platter
Peel And Eat Shrimp • Jumbo Lump Crab Cakes
Island Salad • Short Rib Grilled Cheese

SOME BASICS

SCAN FOR MENU

Reservations:	NO
Spirits:	FULL BAR
Parking:	STREET
Outdoor Dining:	YES

DARUMA JAPANESE STEAK HOUSE

5459 Fruitville Road*
941-342-6600
darumarestaurant.com

FRUITVILLE RD	ASIAN	COST: $$

HOURS: Daily, 5PM to 10PM

WHAT TO EXPECT: Fun Date Night • Good For Kids • Great For Groups
Private Parties

BEST BITES: Gyoza • Negamaki • DaRuMa Teppan Combinations
Sushi • Shrimp Tempura • YoYo Shrimp
Warm & Cold Sake Choices

SOME BASICS

SCAN FOR MENU

Reservations:	YES
Spirits:	FULL BAR
Parking:	LOT
Outdoor Dining:	NO

DEMETRIO'S PIZZERIA

4410 South Tamiami Trail
941-922-1585
demetriospizzeria.com

SOUTH TRAIL	ITALIAN	COST: $$

HOURS: Sun-Thur, 11AM to 8PM
Fri & Sat, 11AM to 8:30PM

WHAT TO EXPECT: Family Pizza Place • Great For A Group
Casual Dining Atmosphere • Lots Of Parking

BEST BITES: Pizza! • Manicotti • Sausage or Meatball Sub
Chicken Parmigiana • "Deep Dish Bake"
Gyro Plate • Greek Salad & Chef Salad

SCAN FOR MENU

SOME BASICS

Reservations:	NO
Spirits:	BEER/WINE
Parking:	LOT
Outdoor Dining:	NO

DER DUTCHMAN

3713 Bahia Vista Street
941-955-8007
dhgroup.com

PINECRAFT	AMISH	COST: $$

HOURS: Mon-Sat, 7AM to 8PM
CLOSED SUNDAY

WHAT TO EXPECT: Good For Kids • Easy On The Wallet
Home Cooking • Great Pie • Groups Welcome

BEST BITES: Roast Beef, Turkey or Meatloaf Manhattan
Homemade Soups • Broasted Chicken • Pie!
Breakfast, Lunch & Dinner Buffet

SCAN FOR MENU

SOME BASICS

Reservations:	NO
Spirits:	NONE
Parking:	LOT
Outdoor Dining:	NO

DIM SUM KING

8194 Tourist Center Drive
941-306-5848
dimsumsarasota.com

LAKEWOOD RANCH	ASIAN	COST: $$

HOURS: Lunch, Wed-Mon,11AM to 2:30PM
Dinner, Wed-Mon, 5PM to 8:30PM • CLOSED TUESDAY

WHAT TO EXPECT: Dim Sum!! • Very Casual Atmosphere
Great For A Quick Lunch • Lots Of Parking Available

BEST BITES: Steamed Spare Ribs in Black Bean Sauce
Chicken ShuMai • Shanghai Style Dumplings
Honey Glazed BBQ Pork • Crispy Shrimp Toast

SOME BASICS

SCAN FOR MENU

Reservations:	NO
Spirits:	BEER/WINE
Parking:	LOT
Outdoor Dining:	NO

DOGGYSTYLE

1544 Main Street
941-260-5835
hotdogswithstyle.com

DOWNTOWN	AMERICAN	COST: $

HOURS: Mon-Sat, 11AM to 6PM
CLOSED SUNDAY

WHAT TO EXPECT: Hot Dogs, Lots Of Them! • Good For Kids
Quick Lunch Spot • Fast, Friendly Service

BEST BITES: Signature Dogs (Chicago, NY, Detroit, KC, California)
Half Pound Burgers! • Chili Cheese Fries
Handspun Shakes

SOME BASICS

SCAN FOR MENU

Reservations:	NO
Spirits:	BEER
Parking:	STREET
Outdoor Dining:	YES

The Colony Restaurant's
Famous Colony Snapper

Created by Michael Klauber, 1980

INGREDIENTS - SNAPPER
4 - 8 oz American red or yellowtail snapper
Salt & black pepper to taste
4 oz olive oil

INGREDIENTS - CRAB MEAT, SUNDRIED TOMATO, AND FRESH BASIL, LEMON BEURRE BLANC
1 shallot, minced
1 cup white wine
3 oz Champagne vinegar
1 cup heavy cream
1 lb unsalted butter, cut into cubes
4 oz lemon juice
4 oz jumbo lump crab meat
3 oz. sun dried tomatoes, julienne
2 oz fresh basil, chiffonade
Salt to taste

METHOD - SNAPPER
Heat Olive oil in heavy skillet pan, season snapper with salt and pepper. Cook the snapper until golden. Turn and continue cooking another 5 minutes. Finish in a 350° oven for about 5-6 minutes.

METHOD - LEMON BEURRE BLANC
Simmer the shallots, wine and vinegar, until reduced ¾ of the way. Add cream and let cook until thicken. Incorporate the butter

with a whisk until fully emulsified. Season with salt, add the sun-dried tomatoes, basil and crabmeat with lemon juice, stir and simmer, place snapper on plate and spoon a generous amount of Beurre Blanc over the top. Your Choice of Starch and Vegetables

Michael became Food & Beverage Director of his family's Colony Beach & Tennis Resort 1980. This was one of the first dishes he added to the restaurant menu – it became a classic at the Colony Restaurant and is now on the menu at Michael's On East!

DOLCE ITALIA
6551 Gateway Avenue
941-921-7007
dolceitaliarestaurant.com

GULF GATE	ITALIAN	COST: $$

HOURS: Mon-Sat, 5PM to 9PM
CLOSED SUNDAY

WHAT TO EXPECT: Great For A Date • Good Wine List
Lots Of Atmosphere • Family Owned

BEST BITES: Burrata • Caprese • Trenne Dolce Italia
Gnocchi Di Patate Al Quatro Formaggi • Lasagna Emiliana
Veal Scallopini • Torte Al Limoncello

SCAN FOR MENU

SOME BASICS
Reservations:	YES
Spirits:	BEER/WINE
Parking:	LOT
Outdoor Dining:	NO

DRIFT KITCHEN
700 Benjamin Franklin Drive (Lido Beach Resort)
941-388-2161
lidobeachresort.com/dining/drift

LIDO KEY	AMERICAN	COST: $$

HOURS: Daily, 7AM to 10PM
Happy Hour Daily, 4PM to 6PM

WHAT TO EXPECT: Upscale Dining • 180° Gulf Views
Lido Beach Resort

BEST BITES: Traditional Eggs Benedict • Cuban Eggs
Crispy Crab Cake • Charcuterie Board • Lido Caesar
Pizza & Flatbreads • Rigatoni Bolognese • Key Lime Pie

SCAN FOR MENU

SOME BASICS

Reservations:	YES
Spirits:	FULL BAR
Parking:	LOT
Outdoor Dining:	NO

DRUNKEN POET CAFÉ
1572 Main Street
941-955-8404
drunkenpoetcafesrq.com

DOWNTOWN	THAI	COST: $$

HOURS: Sun-Thur, 11AM to 10PM
Fri & Sat, 11AM to 12AM

WHAT TO EXPECT: Casual Atmosphere • Good Vegan Options
Later Night Dining • Great For Small Groups

BEST BITES: Pinky In The Blanket • Crispy Duck Basil
Pad Thai • Pad Kee Mao • Thai Spare Ribs
Duck Noodle Soup • Sushi!! • Fried Ice Cream

SCAN FOR MENU

SOME BASICS

Reservations:	YES
Spirits:	BEER/WINE
Parking:	STREET
Outdoor Dining:	YES

DRY DOCK WATERFRONT RESTAURANT

412 Gulf of Mexico Drive (Marker 6 By Boat)
941-383-0102
drydockwaterfrontgrill.com

LONGBOAT KEY	SEAFOOD	COST: $$

HOURS: Sun-Thur, 11AM to 9PM
Fri & Sat, 11AM to 10PM

WHAT TO EXPECT: Great Water View • Local Seafood • Happy Hour
Good For Groups • Opentable Reservations

BEST BITES: Lobster Bites • Oysters Rockefeller • Fishcamp Chowder
Caesar Salad • Linguine with Clams • Boathouse Tacos
Citrus Grouper • Ribeye Steak • Lobster Rolls

SOME BASICS

SCAN FOR MENU

Reservations:	YES
Spirits:	FULL BAR
Parking:	LOT
Outdoor Dining:	YES

DUTCH VALLEY RESTAURANT

6721 South Tamiami Trail
941-924-1770
dutchvalleyrestaurant.net

SOUTH TRAIL	AMERICAN	COST: $$

HOURS: Daily, 7AM to 9PM

WHAT TO EXPECT: Comfort Food • Casual Dining • Est. 1972!
Good For Kids • Early Dining Crowd

BEST BITES: Daily Specials • Homemade Soups • Eggs Benedict
Omelets • Classic French Dip • Sirloin Bacon Burger
BLT • Broasted Chicken! • Lamb Shank • Meat Loaf

SOME BASICS

SCAN FOR MENU

Reservations:	NO
Spirits:	BEER/WINE
Parking:	LOT
Outdoor Dining:	NO

DUVAL'S FRESH. LOCAL. SEAFOOD.

1435 Main Street
941-312-4001
duvalsfreshlocalseafood.com

DOWNTOWN	AMERICAN	COST: $$$

HOURS: Sun-Thur, 11AM to 10PM
Fri & Sat, 11AM to 11PM

WHAT TO EXPECT: Brunch • Opentable Reservations
Great Happy Hour • Free Shuttle To The Restaurant

BEST BITES: Lump Crab Cake • Seafood Bruschetta • Po' Boys!
Duval's BLT • Chicken Cutlet Parmesan • Wedge Salad
Bouillabaisse • Duval's Seafood Sampler • Bread Pudding

SCAN FOR MENU

SOME BASICS

Reservations:	YES
Spirits:	FULL BAR
Parking:	STREET
Outdoor Dining:	YES

EL MELVIN COCINA MEXICANA

1355 Main Street
941-366-1618
elmelvin.com

DOWNTOWN	MEXICAN	COST: $$

HOURS: Sun-Thur, 11AM to 10PM
Fri & Sat, 11AM to 11PM

WHAT TO EXPECT: Casual Mexican Cuisine • Good For Groups
Great Margaritas! • "Mex-Eclectic" • Weekend Brunch

BEST BITES: Fajita's • Queso Fundido • Agua Chile
Enchilada Divorciadas • Combo Platters
Short Rib Birria Chimichanga • Tres Leches

SCAN FOR MENU

SOME BASICS

Reservations:	YES
Spirits:	FULL BAR
Parking:	STREET
Outdoor Dining:	YES

EL TORO BRAVO

3218 Clark Road
941-924-0006
eltorobravosarasota.com

MEXICAN	COST: $$

HOURS: Tue-Thur, 11AM to 8PM • Fri, 11AM to 9PM
Sat, 5PM to 9PM • CLOSED SUNDAY & MONDAY

WHAT TO EXPECT: Great for families • Super casual dining
Usually busy • Online reservations • Lots of parking

BEST BITES: Jalapeños Rellenos • Queso Blanco
Shrimp Chimichanga • Combination Plates
Chips & Homemade Salsa • Deep Fried Cheesecake

SOME BASICS

SCAN FOR MENU

Reservations:	YES
Spirits:	BEER/WINE
Parking:	LOT
Outdoor Dining:	NO

Get Your Sarasota Restaurant News!

FOLLOW, LIKE & SUBSCRIBE!
dineSarasota

EUPHEMIA HAYE

5540 Gulf of Mexico Drive
941-383-3633
euphemiahaye.com

LONGBOAT KEY	AMERICAN	COST: $$$$

HOURS: Tue-Thur, 5:30PM to 9PM • Fri & Sat, 5PM to 9:30PM
Sun, 5:30PM to 9PM • CLOSED MONDAY

WHAT TO EXPECT: Great For A Date • The Haye Loft For Dessert!
Fine Dining Experience • Great For Special Occasions

BEST BITES: Snails Leslie • Classic Caesar Salad
Tagliatelle Alla Carbonara • Roasted Duckling
Euphemia's Prime Peppered Steak • Key West Snapper

SCAN FOR MENU

SOME BASICS

Reservations:	YES
Spirits:	FULL BAR
Parking:	LOT
Outdoor Dining:	NO

1592 WOOD FIRED KITCHEN & COCKTAILS

1592 Main Street
941-365-2234
1592srq.com

DOWNTOWN	GREEK	COST: $$

HOURS: Mon-Thur, 11AM to 10PM • Fri & Sat, 11AM to 11PM
Sun, 4PM to 10PM

WHAT TO EXPECT: Great Casual Dining • Great Happy Hour
Nice Street-Side Dining • Good Downtown Lunch Spot

BEST BITES: Farmers Market Hummus • Saganaki
Spicy Feta Spread • Pulled Lamb Open Faced Pita
Moussaka • Pizza! • Piri Piri Chicken Breast

SCAN FOR MENU

SOME BASICS

Reservations:	YES
Spirits:	BEER/WINE
Parking:	STREET
Outdoor Dining:	YES

481 GOURMET
481 North Orange Avenue
941-362-0400
481gourmetsarasota.com

ROSEMARY DIST	AMERICAN	COST: $$$

HOURS: Wed-Sun, 4PM to 9:30PM • Sunday Brunch, 11AM to 3PM
CLOSED MONDAY & TUESDAY

WHAT TO EXPECT: Great Outdoor Dining Space • Seasonal Menu
Sunday Brunch • Upscale Atmosphere

BEST BITES: Watermelon Basil Salad • 481 Meatball
Italian Pomodoro • Bouillabaisse • Seared Scallops
Osso Bucco Braised Short Rib • Poached Pear

SOME BASICS
SCAN FOR MENU

Reservations:	YES
Spirits:	FULL BAR
Parking:	STREET
Outdoor Dining:	YES

FAICCO'S ITALIAN HERO'S AND GRILL
3590 Webber Street
941-960-1395

NEW

	DELI	COST: $$

HOURS: Sat-Thur, 10:30AM to 6PM • Fri, 10:30AM to 7PM
CLOSED SUNDAY

WHAT TO EXPECT: Good For Families • Perfect For A Quick Lunch
Family Owned & Operated • Super Casual

BEST BITES: Sausage Rolls • Spicy Italian Hero
Muffuletta • Roast Beef Italiano • Chicken Broccoli Rabe
Homemade Porchetta • Grilled Hot Dogs

SOME BASICS
SCAN FOR MENU

Reservations:	No
Spirits:	NONE
Parking:	LOT
Outdoor Dining:	YES

FOR THE FARMERS

By Tracy Freeman, edible Sarasota

Farming is intrinsically about sustaining land, family, and community." —Hal Hamilton

We're blessed in our community with an abundance of opportunities to connect with the farmers, growers, artisans, and chefs that enhance our lives with their offerings. It's a joy to visit one of the farmers' markets around town or to eat a meal at a local restaurant that uses produce from one of the many farms that operate locally. The collaboration between chefs and farmers is a particularly beautiful partnership that we should be proud to celebrate. It is so important not to lose sight of the magic of a true farm-to-table experience. The benefits of eating and shopping locally have been well known for many years and the consequences of not doing so can have negative effects on our health, our economy, and our society.

There is a deep and soulful pleasure to be found in eating food that has been cultivated and prepared by people that you know. This pleasure should not be taken for granted. I love to see chefs honor and respect the ingredients that they source from local farmers, fishers, and growers. Chef Steve Phelps of Indigenous Restaurant often enthuses about the bounty he gets from farms such as the Homestead Hydroponic Farm in Myakka City and Worden Farm in Punta Gorda. Chef Drew Adams and the team at Meliora fill their plates and their Instagram feed with stunning produce from farms like Blumenberry Farms in Sarasota and Harpke Family Farm. Ed Chiles of Chiles Hospitality provides all his restaurants—Beach House, Sandbar, and Mar Vista—with fresh farmed organic produce from Gamble Creek Farms in Parrish.

Chefs are (deservedly) treated with much respect and admiration and are praised and recognized often for their contributions to our communities, but today I'm here to offer a shout-out to the farmers, the growers, and the fishers. Thank you for all that you do, thank you for your passion and your dedication, thank you for providing us all with the fruits (and vegetables) of your labor.

"Agriculture is the greatest and fundamentally the most important of our industries. The cities are but the branches of the tree of national life, the roots of which go deeply into the land. We all flourish or decline with the farmer." —Bernard Baruch

edible Sarasota is a quarterly publication that promotes and celebrates the abundance of local foods and other notable products in the Gulf Coast Region. edible Sarasota is available at no cost in restaurants, hotels, grocers, wine shops, farmers markets, bakeries, coffee shops, boutiques and health complexes throughout Sarasota, Manatee and Charlotte counties. For more information, www.ediblecommunities.com.

FIGARO BISTRO
1944 Hillview Street
941-960-2109
figaro-bistro.com

SOUTHSIDE VILLAGE	FRENCH	COST: $$$

HOURS: Tue-Thur, 5PM to 9PM
Fri & Sat, 5PM to 9:30PM CLOSED SUNDAY & MONDAY

WHAT TO EXPECT: Authentic, Upscale French Cuisine
Nice Wine List • Try The Escargots De Bourgogne

BEST BITES: Escargots Meurette • Salade Lyonnaise
Moules Frites • Boeuf Bourguignon • Filet de Bœuf
Cassoulet Toulousain • Crêpe Suzette

SOME BASICS
Reservations:	YES
Spirits:	BEER/WINE
Parking:	STREET
Outdoor Dining:	YES

SCAN FOR MENU

FINS AT SHARKEY'S

1600 Harbor Drive South
941-999-3467
finsatsharkys.com

VENICE	AMERICAN	COST: $$$

HOURS: Lunch, Daily, 11:45PM to 2:30PM
Dinner, Daily, 4PM to 10PM

WHAT TO EXPECT: Beachfront Dining • "Fins Frenzy" Happy Hour
Good Wine List • "Steakhouse With A Serious Seafood Side"

BEST BITES: Cheese & Charcuterie Plate • Josper Grilled Octopus
Lobster Potato Nachos • Heirloom Tomato Caprese
Smoked Rib Eye • Faroe Island Salmon

SCAN FOR MENU

SOME BASICS

Reservations:	YES
Spirits:	FULL BAR
Parking:	LOT
Outdoor Dining:	YES

FLAVIO'S DOWNTOWN

1766 Main Street
941-960-2305
flaviosonmain.com

DOWNTOWN	ITALIAN	COST: $$$

HOURS: Mon-Thur, 4PM to 9PM • Fri & Sat, 4PM to 9:30PM
CLOSED SUNDAY

WHAT TO EXPECT: Daily Happy Hour • Classic Italian Cuisine
Upscale, Comfortable Atmosphere • Good Wine List

BEST BITES: Fritto Misto • Tuna Tartare • Linguine Carbonara
Agnolotti ai Funghi • Branzino • Veal Osso Buco
Pollo al Milanese

SCAN FOR MENU

SOME BASICS

Reservations:	YES
Spirits:	FULL BAR
Parking:	STREET
Outdoor Dining:	YES

BURGER TIME!
SOME OF SARASOTA'S BEST

Hob Nob Drive-In • 1701 N. Washington Blvd. • 955-5001
WHAT TO EXPECT: Always one of Sarasota's best burger stops. Old school, nothing fancy. The "Hob Nob" burger basket is a must.

Indigenous • 239 S. Links Ave. • 706-4740
WHAT TO EXPECT: This one is always a pleasant surprise. Chef Phelps puts out a delicious burger. Can you say, bacon jam?

Island House Tap & Grill • 5110 Ocean Blvd. • 487-8116
WHAT TO EXPECT: They have a super secret prep method that turns out a perfectly cooked, juicy, and delicious burger every time!

Knick's Tavern & Grill • 1818 S. Osprey Ave. • 955-7761
WHAT TO EXPECT: Known for their burgers. Big and super tasty. For something a little different, try a Brunch Burger. Yep, egg topper.

Made • 1990 Main St. • 953-2900
WHAT TO EXPECT: Niman Ranch beef + billionaire bacon. What more do you really need to say? Delicious! Great sides, too.

Patrick's 1481 • 1481 Main St. • 955-1481
WHAT TO EXPECT: It's all about the burger at Patrick's. This restaurant is a downtown institution. Try it and you'll know why.

Shake Shack • 190 N. Cattlemen Rd. • 413-1351
WHAT TO EXPECT: If you have a Shake Shack in your town/city it has to make your "best of" list. Nothing quite like a ShackBurger.

Shakespeare's • 3550 S. Osprey Ave. • 364-5938
WHAT TO EXPECT: A caramelized onion & Brie burger! English pub atmosphere. Lots and lots of craft beer to wash it all down.

Tasty Home Cookin' • 3854 S. Tuttle Ave. • 921-4969
WHAT TO EXPECT: This one is just a bit different in the burger department. Think White Castle. 3 "Tasty Burgers" for $4.29!!

FLAVIO'S ON SIESTA
5239 Ocean Boulevard
941-349-0995
flaviosbrickovenandbar.com

SIESTA KEY	ITALIAN	COST: $$$

HOURS: Daily, 4PM to 10PM
Happy Hour, 4PM to 6PM

WHAT TO EXPECT: Homemade Italian Cuisine • Brick Oven Pizza
Good Meetup Spot • Siesta Village Location

BEST BITES: Brick Oven Pizza! • Mozzarella in Carrozza
Spiedino Di Gamberi • Burrata e Prosciutto
Insalata Cesare • Pappardelle Ai Porcini • Nodino Di Vitello

SCAN FOR MENU

SOME BASICS
Reservations:	YES
Spirits:	FULL BAR
Parking:	LOT
Outdoor Dining:	YES

FLIRT SUSHI LOUNGE　　　　　　　**NEW**
1296 1st Street
941-343-2122
flirtsushilounge.com

DOWNTOWN	ASIAN	COST: $$$

HOURS: Lunch Daily, 11:30AM to 3PM
Dinner Nightly, 5PM to 2AM

WHAT TO EXPECT: Sushi! • Late Night Dining
Great Downtown Location • Perfect After A Show Or Concert

BEST BITES: Dirty Seaweed Salad • Tuna Tostones
Andaluzian Gazpacho • Sashimi • Nigiri

SCAN FOR MENU

SOME BASICS
Reservations:	YES
Spirits:	FULL BAR
Parking:	STREET
Outdoor Dining:	YES

FOOD & BEER

6528 Superior Avenue*
941-952-3361
eatfooddrinkbeer.com

GULF GATE	AMERICAN	COST: $$

HOURS: Mon-Thur, 11AM to 1AM • Fri, 11AM to 2AM
Sat, 10AM to 2AM • Sun, 10AM to 1AM

WHAT TO EXPECT: Super Casual • Good Local Beer Selection
Later Night Menu • Sat. & Sun. Brunch

BEST BITES: Down The Hatch Burger • Malibu Barbie Wrap
Birria Tacos • Cali Hot Cobb Bowl • Fries Goat Cheese
Buffalo Chicken Wedge • Red Velvet Oreos

SOME BASICS

SCAN FOR MENU

Reservations:	NO
Spirits:	BEER/WINE
Parking:	STREET/LOT
Outdoor Dining:	NO

FORK & HEN

`NEW`

2801 North Tamiami Trail
941-960-1212
forkandhenssrq.com

NORTH TRAIL	AMERICAN	COST: $$

HOURS: Tues-Thur, 11:30AM to 7:30PM • Fri-Sun, 11:30AM to 8PM
CLOSED MONDAY

WHAT TO EXPECT: Chef Driven Menu • Super Casual Dining
Scratch Kitchen • Ringling School Neighborhood

BEST BITES: Creole Brussels & Cauliflower • Chicken Parm
El Chido Hot Chicken Sandwich • The Hitman Burger
Watermelon & Feta Salad • Chicken & Waffles

SOME BASICS

SCAN FOR MENU

Reservations:	NO
Spirits:	NONE
Parking:	LOT
Outdoor Dining:	YES

FRESH START CAFE

630 South Orange Avenue
941-373-1242
freshstartcafesrq.com

BURNS COURT	AMERICAN	COST: $$

HOURS: Thur-Mon, 9AM to 2PM
CLOSED TUESDAY & WEDNESDAY

WHAT TO EXPECT: Great For Outdoor Dining • Breakfast & Lunch
Very Casual • Lots of Parking • Eclectic Menu

BEST BITES: ShakShuka • Bagel & Lox • Frittatas
Cinnamon Raisin French Toast • Thanksgiving Day Sandwich
Reubens • Lemon-Herb Salmon Salad • French Press Coffee

SCAN FOR MENU

SOME BASICS

Reservations:	NO
Spirits:	BEER/WINE
Parking:	LOT
Outdoor Dining:	YES

FUSHIPOKE

128 North Orange Avenue
941-330-1795
fushipoke.com

DOWNTOWN	HAWAIIAN	COST: $$

HOURS: Mon-Sat, 11AM to 8PM
CLOSED SUNDAY

WHAT TO EXPECT: Super Casual • Fantastic For A Quick Lunch
Easy On The Wallet • Happy Hour Sake Shots!

BEST BITES: Build Your Own Poke Bowl • Spicy Poke Bowl
Tonkotsu Ramen • Pork Belly Steamed Buns
Iced Green Tea • Kombucha

SCAN FOR MENU

SOME BASICS

Reservations:	NO
Spirits:	BEER/WINE
Parking:	STREET
Outdoor Dining:	NO

GECKO'S GRILL & PUB
6606 South Tamiami Trail*
941-248-2020
geckosgrill.com

SOUTH TRAIL	AMERICAN	COST: $$

HOURS: Daily, 11AM to 10PM

WHAT TO EXPECT: Great To Watch A Game • Yelp Waitlist
Good Burgers • "American Pub Food"

BEST BITES: Blue Cheese Chips • Loaded Potato Scoops
Wings! • Black Beans & Rice • The Ultimate Cobb
Flatbreads • Wraps • Burgers • Cuban Sub

SOME BASICS

SCAN FOR MENU

Reservations:	NO
Spirits:	FULL BAR
Parking:	LOT
Outdoor Dining:	YES

GENTILE BROTHERS CHEESESTEAKS
7523 South Tamiami Trail
941-926-0441
gentilesteaks.com

SOUTH TRAIL	AMERICAN	COST: $

HOURS: Mon-Sat, 11AM to 7PM
CLOSED SUNDAY

WHAT TO EXPECT: Philly Experience • No Frills Dining
Easy On The Wallet • Family Owned • Good For Kids

BEST BITES: Clemenza Cheesesteak Sandwich • Italian Hoagie
South Philly Sandwich • Cheese Fries

SCAN FOR MENU

SOME BASICS

Reservations:	NO
Spirits:	NONE
Parking:	LOT
Outdoor Dining:	NO

GILLIGAN'S ISLAND BAR

5253 Ocean Boulevard
941-346-8122
gilligansislandbar.com

SIESTA KEY	AMERICAN	COST: $$

HOURS: Sun-Thur, 11AM to 11PM
Fri & Sat, 11AM to 12AM

WHAT TO EXPECT: Siesta Village • Live Music • Younger Crowd
Fun Weekend Hangout Place

BEST BITES: Jumbo Peel & Eat Shrimp • Beach House Salad
Big Kahuna Burger • Chicken Ranch Wrap
Gilligan's Queso Dip • Key Lime Pie

SCAN FOR MENU

SOME BASICS

Reservations:	NO
Spirits:	FULL BAR
Parking:	STREET
Outdoor Dining:	YES

GOOD LIQUID BREWING   **NEW**

1570 Lakefront Drive
941-238-6466
goodliquidbrewingcompany.com

WATERSIDE PLACE	BREW PUB	COST: $$

HOURS: Sun-Thur, 11AM to 9PM
Fri & Sat, 11AM to 10PM

WHAT TO EXPECT: Brew Pub • Fantastic Outdoor Gathering Area
Busy On Weekends

BEST BITES: GLB Pretzel • Shrimp & Crab Cakes
BBQ Chicken Salad • The Hay Stack Burger
GL Double Stack Burger • Wood Grilled "Brewzettas"

SCAN FOR MENU

SOME BASICS

Reservations:	NO
Spirits:	FULL BAR
Parking:	STREET
Outdoor Dining:	YES

GRANDPA'S SCHNITZEL

`NEW`

2700 Stickney Point Road
941-922-3888
grandpas-schnitzel.com

GERMAN	COST: $$

HOURS: Mon-Sat, 8AM to 1:30PM • Mon-Sat, 5PM to 9PM
CLOSED SUNDAY

WHAT TO EXPECT: Real German Cuisine • Family Owned
Schnitzels! • Lots Of Parking

BEST BITES: "Schnitzel-Burgers" • Currywurst • Schweinbraten
Bratwurst • German Apple Strudel • Pfannkuchen

SOME BASICS

SCAN FOR MENU

Reservations:	YES
Spirits:	BEER/WINE
Parking:	LOT
Outdoor Dining:	NO

THE GRASSHOPPER

7253 South Tamiami Trail
941-923-3688
thegrasshoppertexmex.com

SOUTH TRAIL	MEXICAN	COST: $$

HOURS: Mon-Sat, 11AM to 10PM
Happy Hour, 3:30PM to 5:30PM

WHAT TO EXPECT: Easy On The Wallet • Happy Hour
Good Cocktail Selection • Good For Groups

BEST BITES: Huevos Rancheros • Signature Queso • Guacamole
Combination Plate • Taco Plate • Tamale Plate
Veggie Chili Rellenos • Menudo

SOME BASICS

SCAN FOR MENU

Reservations:	YES
Spirits:	FULL BAR
Parking:	LOT
Outdoor Dining:	NO

VEGETARIAN OR VEGAN?
HERE ARE SARASOTA'S BEST PLACES

Vegetarian and vegan lifestyles both offer a healthy way of eating. But, as any one who keeps either of these diets knows, dining out can sometimes be more than a challenge. I mean, how many grilled cheese sandwiches can one person consume? Don't despair. We're here to help. Sarasota has its share of options for those who choose a meat-free existence. Keep in mind that the places listed below may not be strictly vegan/veg only. But, they will offer some nice menu options.

Beauty of Sprouts • 433 N. Orange Ave. • 350-8449
THE HIGHLIGHTS: "Made From Scratch" kitchen. Organic, gluten free, GMO free cuisine. Not open every day. Check for days.

Ka Papa Cuisine • 1830 S. Osprey Ave. • 600-8590
THE HIGHLIGHTS: Sarasota's only 100% plant-based and vegan full service restaurant. Excellent menu of large and small plates.

Lila • 1576 Main St. • 296-1042
THE HIGHLIGHTS: Named one of the best vegetarian restaurants in the country by OpenTable. Refined vegetarian cuisine.

Screaming Goat Taqueria • 6606 Superior Ave. • 210-3992
THE HIGHLIGHTS: Tacos, bowls, and more. Lots of vegan/veg options here. Your non-veg friends will be super happy, too!

Spice Station • 1438 Boulevard of the Arts • 343-2894
THE HIGHLIGHTS: Fantastic Thai cuisine. They've got a large section of vegetarian dishes on their menu. Cozy dining space.

Veg • 6538 Gateway Ave. • 312-6424
THE HIGHLIGHTS: The name says it best. Vegetarian + seafood. Dozens of their dishes can be made vegan too. Delicious!

GRAZE STREET AMI

3218 E. Bay Drive
941-896-6320
grazestreetami.com

NEW

HOLMES BEACH	AMERICAN	COST: $

HOURS: Wed-Fri, 11AM to 6PM • Sat, 10AM to 6PM
Sun, 10AM to 3PM • CLOSED MONDAY & TUESDAY

WHAT TO EXPECT: Bakery & Gourmet Shop • Super Casual
Limited Sandwich Menu

BEST BITES: Caprese Sandwich • Green Goddess Sandwich
Beachy BLT • Tuna Salad • Cookies Every Day!

SOME BASICS

SCAN FOR MENU

Reservations:	NO
Spirits:	NONE
Parking:	STREET
Outdoor Dining:	NO

GROVE

10670 Boardwalk Loop
941-893-4321
grovelwr.com

LAKEWOOD RANCH	AMERICAN	COST: $$$

HOURS: Mon-Thur, 11:30AM to 10PM • Fri, 11:30AM to 10:30PM
Sat, 10AM to 10:30PM • Sun, 10AM to 10PM

WHAT TO EXPECT: Happy Hour • Culinary Cocktails
Weekend Brunch 10AM to 3PM • Wine Dinners

BEST BITES: Mussels & Blue • Thai Cauliflower • Tuna Nachos
Flatbreads • NE Clam Chowder • Baby Wedge Salad
Jambalaya • Sushi • Grouper Oscar • Pork Osso Bucco

SOME BASICS

SCAN FOR MENU

Reservations:	YES
Spirits:	FULL BAR
Parking:	LOT
Outdoor Dining:	YES

HARRY'S CONTINENTAL KITCHENS

525 St. Judes Drive
941-383-0777
harryskitchen.com

LONGBOAT KEY	AMERICAN	COST: $$$

HOURS: Restaurant - Daily, 9AM to 9PM
Deli - 11AM to 7PM

WHAT TO EXPECT: Great For A Date • Monthly Wine Events
Upscale Florida Dining • Visit The "Corner Store"

BEST BITES: Shrimp-Cargot • Harry's Famous Crab Cakes
Fresh Chunky Gazpacho • Sautéed Veal Medallions
Roast Maple Leaf Half Duckling • Peanut Butter Pie

SCAN FOR MENU

SOME BASICS

Reservations:	YES
Spirits:	FULL BAR
Parking:	LOT
Outdoor Dining:	YES

HOB NOB DRIVE-IN RESTAURANT

1701 North Washington Boulevard (301 & 17th St.)
941-955-5001
hobnobdrivein.com

DOWNTOWN	AMERICAN	COST: $

HOURS: Mon-Sat, 7AM to 8PM
Sun, 8AM to 4PM

WHAT TO EXPECT: Easy On The Wallet • Fun! • Great For Kids
Sarasota's Oldest Drive-In. • Great Burger!

BEST BITES: Hob Nob Burger • Patty Melt • Chili Cheese Dog
Grilled Ham & Cheese • Tuna Melt • Fried Mushrooms
Onion Rings • Ice Cream Floats!

SCAN FOR MENU

SOME BASICS

Reservations:	NO
Spirits:	BEER/WINE
Parking:	LOT
Outdoor Dining:	YES

THE HUB BAJA GRILL

5148 Ocean Boulevard
941-349-6800
thehubsiestakey.com

SIESTA KEY	AMERICAN	COST: $$

HOURS: Sun-Thur, 11AM to 10PM • Fri & Sat, 11AM to 11PM

WHAT TO EXPECT: Island Dining Experience • Good For Families
Busy In Season • Live Music Daily • Happy Hour Specials

BEST BITES: The Hub Margarita • Lobster Bisque • Baja Salad
Grande Nachos • Mahi Lettuce Wrap • The Hub Cuban
Short Rib Taco Sofrito • Baby Back Ribs

SOME BASICS

SCAN FOR MENU

Reservations:	NO
Spirits:	FULL BAR
Parking:	STREET
Outdoor Dining:	YES

IL PANIFICIO

1703 Main Street*
941-921-5570
panificiousa.com

DOWNTOWN	ITALIAN	COST: $$

HOURS: Daily, 10AM to 9PM

WHAT TO EXPECT: Great For Lunch • Easy On The Wallet
Family Friendly• Nice Spot For A Lunch Meet Up

BEST BITES: Eggplant Rollatini • Italian Salad • Prosciutto Sub
Meatball Parm Sandwich • Pizza By The Slice
Stromboli • Sausage Pepper & Onion Sandwich

SOME BASICS

SCAN FOR MENU

Reservations:	NO
Spirits:	BEER/WINE
Parking:	STREET
Outdoor Dining:	YES

INDIGENOUS RESTAURANT

239 South Links Avenue
941-706-4740
indigenoussarasota.com

TOWLES CT	AMERICAN	COST: $$$

HOURS: Tues-Sat, 5:30PM to 8:30PM
CLOSED SUNDAY & MONDAY

WHAT TO EXPECT: Great For A Date • Fine Dining, Casual Feel
Towles Court Neighborhood • Limited Outdoor Seating

BEST BITES: Wild Mushroom Bisque • Red Curry Fish Dip
Cobia Crudo • Pork Funchi • My Uncle's Burger
Everglades Baked Shrimp & Scallops • Buttermilk Pie

SCAN FOR MENU

SOME BASICS

Reservations:	YES
Spirits:	BEER/WINE
Parking:	LOT/STREET
Outdoor Dining:	YES

INKAWASI PERUVIAN RESTAURANT

10667 Boardwalk Loop
941-360-1110
inkawasirestaurant.com

LAKEWOOD RANCH	PERUVIAN	COST: $$

HOURS: Mon-Thur & Sun, 12PM to 9PM
Fri & Sat, 12PM to 10PM • Sun, 12PM to 8PM

WHAT TO EXPECT: Casual Dining Atmosphere • Tapas Happy Hour
Lakewood Ranch Main Street Location

BEST BITES: Chicharron de Calamar • Empanadas • Ceviche Clásico
Ceviche al Olivo • Inka's Salad • Arroz Chaufa
Lomo Saltado • Duo Marino • Grouper a lo Macho

SCAN FOR MENU

SOME BASICS

Reservations:	YES
Spirits:	BEER/WINE
Parking:	LOT/STREET
Outdoor Dining:	NO

ISLAND HOUSE TAP & GRILL

5110 Ocean Boulevard
941-487-8116
islandhousetapandgrill.com

SIESTA KEY	AMERICAN	COST: $$

HOURS: Daily, 11AM to 10PM

WHAT TO EXPECT: Great Craft Beers • Fantastic Burgers & Tacos
Outdoor Patio • Local Favorite • Daily Specials

BEST BITES: Duck Fat Fries • Chicken Lollipops • Guac n' Chips
Endless Summer Salad • Carnitas Bowl
Carne Asada Tacos • Steakhouse Burger

SOME BASICS

Reservations:	NONE
Spirits:	BEER/WINE
Parking:	LOT
Outdoor Dining:	YES

SCAN FOR MENU

2023 SARASOTA FOOD EVENTS

FORKS & CORKS

WHEN: April 20-24
WHAT: Sponsored by the Sarasota-Manatee Originals. Super popular food event! Wine dinners, seminars, AND the Grand Tasting. A must for Sarasota foodies. Tickets go very fast.
INFO: eatlikealocal.com/forksandcorks

FLORIDA WINEFEST & AUCTION

WHEN: TBD
WHAT: This charity event has been providing needed help to local children's programs for over 30 years. In the past couple of years, because of COVID, there has been an online auction.
INFO: floridawinefest.org

SAVOR SARASOTA RESTAURANT WEEK

WHEN: June 1-14th
WHAT: This restaurant week spans TWO full weeks. It features lots of popular restaurants and showcases three course menus.
INFO: savorsarasota.com

ISLAND HOUSE TAQUERIA

2773 Bee Ridge Road
941-922-8226
islandhousetaqueria.com

MEXICAN	**COST: $$**

HOURS: Daily, 11AM to 10PM

WHAT TO EXPECT: Great Tacos! • Super Casual Atmosphere
Authentic Al Pastor Tacos • Good Craft Beer Selection

BEST BITES: Pork Al Pastor • Aguacate • Birria • Cochinita Pibil
Everything Can Be Made Into: Taco, Burrito, Bowl, Nachos
Tostones, Chimichanga and Quesadilla

SCAN FOR MENU

SOME BASICS

Reservations:	NO
Spirits:	BEER/WINE
Parking:	LOT
Outdoor Dining:	YES

JACK DUSTY

1111 Ritz-Carlton Drive
941-309-2266
ritzcarlton.com/en/hotels/florida/sarasota/dining/jack-dusty

DOWNTOWN	**SEAFOOD**	**COST: $$$**

HOURS: Breakfast, lunch, and dinner daily

WHAT TO EXPECT: Walking Distance To Downtown • Water View
Handmade Cocktails • Opentable Reservations

BEST BITES: Smoked Fish Dip • Sarasota Cioppino • Lobster Roll
Jack's Fish Tacos • South Indian Style Vegetable Curry
Summer Garden Salad • Roasted Grouper

SCAN FOR MENU

SOME BASICS

Reservations:	YES
Spirits:	FULL BAR
Parking:	VALET
Outdoor Dining:	YES

JERSEY GIRL BAGELS

5275 University Parkway
941-388-8910
jerseygirlbagels.net

NEW

UNIVERSITY PARK	DELI	COST: $$

HOURS: Wed-Sun, 7AM to 2PM
CLOSED MONDAY & TUESDAY

WHAT TO EXPECT: NY Style Bagels • Buy One Or A Dozen!
Super Casual • Lots Of Parking • Good For A Carryout

BEST BITES: Egg Salad Sandwich • Lox & Bagel Sandwich
Black & White Cookies • Breakfast Sandwiches

SOME BASICS

SCAN FOR MENU

Reservations:	NO
Spirits:	NONE
Parking:	LOT
Outdoor Dining:	NO

JOEY D'S CHICAGO STYLE EATERY

3811 Kenny Drive*
941-378-8900
joeydsfl.com

	AMERICAN	COST: $$

HOURS: Daily, 11AM to 10PM

WHAT TO EXPECT: Chicago Style Food • Family Friendly
Multiple Locations • Super Casual

BEST BITES: World Famous Chicago Pizza • Stromboli
The Shroom Burger • Original "Chicago Style" Hot Dog
Grilled Maxwell Street Polish • Italian Beef

SOME BASICS

SCAN FOR MENU

Reservations:	NO
Spirits:	BEER/WINE
Parking:	LOT
Outdoor Dining:	YES

JPAN RESTAURANT & SUSHI BAR

3800 South Tamiami Trail (Shops at Siesta Row)*
941-954-5726
jpanrestaurant.com

SHOPS AT SIESTA ROW	JAPANESE	COST: $$

HOURS: Lunch, Mon-Fri, 11:30AM to 2PM
Mon-Sat, 5PM to 9:30PM • Sun, 5PM to 9PM

WHAT TO EXPECT: Great For A Date • Big Sushi Menu
Great Lunch Combos • Opentable Reservations

BEST BITES: Sushi • Sashimi • Bento Boxes • Pork Dumplings
Kfc (Korean Fried Chicken) • Hamachi Chilli
Ramen • Volcano Chicken

SCAN FOR MENU

SOME BASICS

Reservations:	YES
Spirits:	BEER/WINE
Parking:	LOT
Outdoor Dining:	YES

JR'S OLD PACKINGHOUSE CAFE

987 South Packinghouse Drive
941-371-9358
packinghousecafe.com

	AMERICAN	COST: $$

HOURS: Mon-Thur, 11AM to 9PM • Fri & Sat, 11AM to 10PM
CLOSED SUNDAY

WHAT TO EXPECT: Fun For A Date • Live Music
Great Burgers & Cuban Sandwiches

BEST BITES: Queso Burger • Cuban Sandwich OPC Style
Mediterranean Salad • Ropa Vieja • OPC Shrimp
Country Fried Chicken • Key Lime Pie

SCAN FOR MENU

SOME BASICS

Reservations:	NO
Spirits:	FULL BAR
Parking:	LOT
Outdoor Dining:	YES

KA PAPA CUISINE
1830 South Osprey Avenue
941-600-8590
kapapacuisine.com

SOUTHSIDE VILLAGE	VEGAN	COST: $$$

HOURS: Wed-Sun, 5PM to 9PM

WHAT TO EXPECT: 100% Plant Based Cuisine • Vegan
Casual "Urban" Feel • Southside Village Location

BEST BITES: Spicy Edamame • Baked "Feta" • Grilled "Caesar" Salad
Plum-Miso Glazed Eggplant • Pan Roasted Mushrooms
House-Made Pasta With Walnut Pesto

SOME BASICS
SCAN FOR MENU

Reservations:	YES
Spirits:	BEER/WINE
Parking:	LOT/STREET
Outdoor Dining:	YES

KACEY'S SEAFOOD & MORE
4904 Fruitville Road
941-378-3644
kaceysseafood.com

	SEAFOOD	COST: $$

HOURS: Mon-Sat, 11AM to 8PM
CLOSED SUNDAY

WHAT TO EXPECT: Great Affordable Seafood • Good For Families
Casual Dining • Lots Of parking

BEST BITES: Shrimp Scargot • Big Bang Shrimp • Lobster Bisque
Fresh Market Fish • Fish N' Chips • Fried Clam Strips
Tuna "Master Jessie" • Shrimp Trio Dinner

SOME BASICS
SCAN FOR MENU

Reservations:	NO
Spirits:	BEER/WINE
Parking:	LOT
Outdoor Dining:	NO

KIYOSHI SUSHI

6550 Gateway Avenue
941-924-3781

GULF GATE	SUSHI	COST: $$

HOURS: Tues-Sat, 5:30PM to 9PM
CLOSED SUNDAY & MONDAY

WHAT TO EXPECT: Traditional Sushi • Casual & Comfortable
Beautiful Presentations

BEST BITES: Maki Rolls • Chicken Katsu • Sashimi Combo
Chirashi Bowl • Hot & Cold Sake • Green Tea Ice Cream

SCAN FOR MENU

SOME BASICS

Reservations:	YES
Spirits:	BEER/WINE
Parking:	STREET/LOT
Outdoor Dining:	NO

KNICK'S TAVERN & GRILL

1818 South Osprey Avenue
941-955-7761
knickstavernandgrill.com

SOUTHSIDE VILLAGE	AMERICAN	COST: $$

HOURS: Mon-Thur, 11:30AM to 9PM • Fri, 11:30AM to 10PM
Sat, 5PM to 10PM • CLOSED SUNDAY

WHAT TO EXPECT: Casual Dining • Busy In Season • Family Owned
Local Favorite • Great Burgers • Daily Specials

BEST BITES: The Ultimate Wedge • Blackened Calamari
Chipotle Crumbled Bleu Cheese Burger • Mussels
Knickole's Chicken Sandwich • Dessert Specials

SCAN FOR MENU

SOME BASICS

Reservations:	YES
Spirits:	BEER/WINE
Parking:	STREET
Outdoor Dining:	YES

KOJO

1289 North Palm Avenue
941-536-9717
eatkojo.com

DOWNTOWN	ASIAN	COST: $$$

HOURS: Sun-Thur, 4PM to 11PM
Fri & Sat, 4PM to 12AM

WHAT TO EXPECT: Upscale Asian Cuisine • Ramen, Sushi & Bao Buns
Next To Palm Ave Garage • Online Reservations

BEST BITES: Wasabi Caesar Salad • Crispy Tofu Bites
Truffled Chicken Wontons • Torched Salmon Nori Taco
Bao Buns • Wagyu Skirt Steak • Sushi

SOME BASICS

SCAN FOR MENU

Reservations:	YES
Spirits:	FULL BAR
Parking:	GARAGE/STREET
Outdoor Dining:	YES

KORÊ STEAKHOUSE

NEW

1561 Lakefront Drive
941-928-5673
koresteakhouse.com

WATERSIDE PLACE	KOREAN	COST: $$$

HOURS: Open Daily, Lunch & Dinner

WHAT TO EXPECT: REAL Korean Bbq • Super Upscale Feel
Busy For Dinner • Fun For Groups

BEST BITES: Bulgogi Mandoo • Egg Souffle • Japchae Noodles
Dolsot Bibimbap • Kimchi Jjigae • Cheese Corn
Beef, Pork, Seafood, Chicken & Veggie Grilling Items

SOME BASICS

SCAN FOR MENU

Reservations:	NONE
Spirits:	BEER/WINE
Parking:	STREET
Outdoor Dining:	NO

THE LAZY LOBSTER

5350 Gulf of Mexico Drive
941-383-0440
lazylobsteroflongboat.com

LONGBOAT KEY	SEAFOOD	COST: $$$

HOURS: Mon-Sat, 11AM to 9PM
CLOSED SUNDAY

WHAT TO EXPECT: Great Casual Seafood • Early Dining Menu

BEST BITES: Chilled Ahi Tuna • Lobster Scargot • Lobster Bisque
Hot Fried Chicken Salad • The Open Faced Reuben
Stuffed Shrimp "Norma" • Lobster Mac & Cheese

SCAN FOR MENU

SOME BASICS

Reservations:	YES
Spirits:	FULL BAR
Parking:	LOT
Outdoor Dining:	YES

LIBBY'S NEIGHBORHOOD BRASSERIE

1917 South Osprey Avenue*
941-487-7300
libbysneighborhoodbrasserie.com

SOUTHSIDE VILLAGE	AMERICAN	COST: $$$

HOURS: Sun-Thur, 11AM to 9PM
Fri & Sat, 11AM to 10PM

WHAT TO EXPECT: Upscale Dining Experience • Good Wine List
Busy Bar Scene • Reservations A Must During Season

BEST BITES: Tuna Taki • Avocado Eggrolls • Kale Caesar Salad
Krabby Patty Sandwich • Meatball Smash Sandwich
Louisiana Chicken Pasta • Dr. Pepper Ribs

SCAN FOR MENU

SOME BASICS

Reservations:	YES
Spirits:	FULL BAR
Parking:	LOT/STREET
Outdoor Dining:	YES

LILA
1576 Main Street
941-296-1042
lilasrq.com

DOWNTOWN	AMERICAN	COST: $$

HOURS: Mon-Fri, 11AM to 9PM • Sat, 10:30AM to 9PM
CLOSED SUNDAY

WHAT TO EXPECT: Organic, Locally Sourced Menu • Lighter Fare
Opentable Reservations • Lots Of Veg/Vegan Options

BEST BITES: Vegan Sushi Rolls • Roasted Yam Wedges
Red Beet, Apple, Orange Salad • Mushroom Burger
Ramen Noodle Bowl • Verlasso Salmon

SOME BASICS
SCAN FOR MENU

Reservations:	YES
Spirits:	BEER/WINE
Parking:	STREET
Outdoor Dining:	NO

LITTLE SAIGON BISTRO
2725 South Beneva Road
941-312-4730

	VIETNAMESE	COST: $$

HOURS: Tue-Sat 10AM to 8PM
CLOSED SUNDAY & MONDAY

WHAT TO EXPECT: Simple Menu Of Vietnamese Dishes
Lots Of Parking • Great For A Casual Lunch Or Dinner

BEST BITES: Rice Vermicelli • Shrimp & Pork Spring Rolls
Pho Noodle Bowls • Grilled Chicken with Rice

SOME BASICS
SCAN FOR INFO

Reservations:	NO
Spirits:	BEER/WINE
Parking:	LOT
Outdoor Dining:	NO

LOBSTER POT

5157 Ocean Boulevard
941-349-2323
sarasotalobsterpot.com

SIESTA KEY	SEAFOOD	COST: $$

HOURS: Mon-Thur, 11:30AM to 9PM • Fri & Sat, 11:30AM to 9:30PM
CLOSED SUNDAY

WHAT TO EXPECT: Great For Families • Lobster ++ • Siesta Village
Good For Kids

BEST BITES: Kettle of Mussels • Broiled Fiery Scallops
Portuguese Soup • Watermelon Salad • Lazy Dutchess
Alaskan King Crab • Salmon Rockefeller • Filet Mignon

SCAN FOR MENU

SOME BASICS

Reservations:	6 OR MORE
Spirits:	BEER/WINE
Parking:	VALET/STREET
Outdoor Dining:	YES

LOBSTERCRAFT

NEW

St. Armands Circle
941-346-6325
lobstercraft.com

ST ARMANDS	SEAFOOD	COST: $$$

HOURS: Tues-Sun, 11AM to 8PM
CLOSED MONDAY

WHAT TO EXPECT: Super Casual Atmosphere • Great For A Carryout
Busy Area During Season

BEST BITES: Lobster Bisque • Clam Chowder • Lobster Tacos
Lots of Lobster Roll Choices • Lobster Mac n Cheese

SCAN FOR MENU

SOME BASICS

Reservations:	NONE
Spirits:	BEER/WINE
Parking:	STREET/GARAGE
Outdoor Dining:	YES

LOVELY SQUARE
6559 Gateway Avenue
941-724-2512
lovelysquareflorida.com

GULF GATE	AMERICAN	COST: $$

HOURS: Mon-Sun, 8AM to 2PM
CLOSED TUESDAY

WHAT TO EXPECT: Casual Dining Spot • Nice Selection Of Crepes
Good For Families • Easy On The Wallet

BEST BITES: Classic Eggs Benedict • Omelets & Frittatas
Morning Crepe • Banana Nut Pancakes
Greek Salad • Club B.E.L.T. • Baguette Brie Chicken

SOME BASICS
Reservations:	NO
Spirits:	BEER/WINE
Parking:	LOT
Outdoor Dining:	NO

SCAN FOR MENU

MADE
1990 Main Street
941-953-2900
maderestaurant.com

DOWNTOWN	AMERICAN	COST: $$

HOURS: Tue-Fri, Lunch, 11:30AM to 2:30PM • Sun, 10AM to 2PM
Tue-Sat, Dinner, 5PM to 10PM • CLOSED MONDAY

WHAT TO EXPECT: Great For A Date • Upscale, American Cuisine
Chef Driven Menu

BEST BITES: Pork Wings • Disco Fries • MADE Mac-n-Cheese
Smoked Chicken Taco Salad • "Four" Meatloaf
MADE Burger • Short Rib Philly • Nashville Hot Chicken

SOME BASICS
Reservations:	YES
Spirits:	FULL BAR
Parking:	STREET/GARAGE
Outdoor Dining:	YES

SCAN FOR MENU

Beef Burgundy

Mademoiselle Paris

INGREDIENTS
1 KG of beef for boeuf bourguignon
2 TBSP of flour
3 carrots
1 onion
1 garlic head
1 branch of celery
1 bottle of wine (from Burgundy if possible)
1L of sparkling water (Perrier, San Pellegrino…)
2 whole thyme sprigs
1 bay leaf

METHOD - MARINADE
1. Remove all bone cartilage, skin and fat. Put them all in a pan with butter in order to caramelize them. Sprinkle with water in order to obtain a "cooking jus "
2. Cut the beef into 5cm pieces
3. Marinade the meat in sparkling water for 1 hour
4. Then, marinade the meat in red wine for 1 hour
5. Peel and chop the onions and carrots
6. Prepare the aromatic garnish with thyme, bay leaf, garlic, carrots and celery
7. Add to the marinade the aromatic garnish, carrots and celery
8. Drain and dry the meat in a dishcloth
9. Filter the wine and the aromatic garnish. Separate the meat from the aromatic garnish and keep the wine.

METHOD - COOKING
1. Melt the butter and olive oil in a large skillet and fry the meat
2. Add the aromatic garnish from the marinade
3. Coat with flour the meat
4. Add the wine from the marinade and flambé the meat

5. Add the "cooking jus"
6. Put the lid and place during 2 hours in the oven with 200°C

CHEFS TIP: We marinade the meat in sparkling water for one hour because the bicarbonate naturally present in sparkling water will tenderize the meat. Sparkling water will melt the collagen (protein content of meat) and the meat will be more flavorful and tender with less fat.

You can add a square of dark chocolate in your preparation to adjust the acidity of the wine and add more taste to your beef burgundy.

Mademoiselle Paris is a family owned restaurant since 2016 and an authentic French restaurant and bakery. Enjoy the taste of authentic French bistro cuisine for breakfast, lunch or dinner. Our executive Chef prepare a large variety of traditional dishes : mussels & French fries, beef burgundy, foie gras, snails,…. Mademoiselle Paris has now 3 locations : Downtown Sarasota | Anna Maria Island | UTC. Learn more at mademoiselleparis.com

MADEMOISELLE PARIS
8527 Cooper Creek Boulevard*
941-355-2323
mademoiselleparis.com

LWR	FRENCH	COST: $$

HOURS: Mon & Tue, 7:45AM to 5PM
Wed-Sun, 7:45AM to 9PM

WHAT TO EXPECT: Traditional French Fare • Casual European Dining
Tartines, Omlettes And More!

BEST BITES: Tartine Gourmande • Omelettes • Quiche Lorraine
Croque Madame • Beef Burgundy • French Onion Soup
Crepes! • Profiteroles • Crême Brulée

SOME BASICS

Reservations:	YES
Spirits:	BEER/WINE
Parking:	LOT
Outdoor Dining:	YES

SCAN FOR MENU

SARASOTA MARKETS AND SPECIALTY STORES

A Taste of Europe • 2130 Gulf Gate Dr. • 921-9084
WHAT YOU CAN FIND THERE: Foods from twenty different European countries. Fresh deli, specialty cheeses, beer, wine, and more.

Alpine Steakhouse • 4520 S. Tamiami Trl. • 922-3797
WHAT YOU CAN FIND THERE: Meat market. Skilled butchers, super helpful. Famous for Turducken. Also, full service restaurant.

Artisan Cheese Company • 550 Central Ave. • 951-7860
WHAT YOU CAN FIND THERE: Cheese store. Hard to find small domestic dairies. Lunch menu. Classes. Knowledgeable staff.

Big Water Fish Market • 6641 Midnight Pass Rd. • 554-8101
WHAT YOU CAN FIND THERE: Fresh Florida fish. Great prepared seafood items. Just south of Siesta Key's south bridge.

The Butcher's Block • 3242 17th St. • 955-2822
WHAT YOU CAN FIND THERE: Meat market/butcher shop. Custom cuts, prime meats. Good wine selection. They have gift baskets.

Butcher's Mark • 8519 Cooper Creek Blvd. • 358-6328
WHAT YOU CAN FIND THERE: Sustainable beef. Lots of marinades and pre-marinaded meat. Charcuterie and antipasto.

Casa Italia • 2080 Constitution Blvd. • 924-1179
WHAT YOU CAN FIND THERE: A wide variety of hard to find ethnic items. Cheeses, deli, & more. Cooking classes. Prepared foods.

Geier's Sausage Kitchen • 7447 S. Tamiami Trl. • 923-3004
WHAT YOU CAN FIND THERE: Sausage & more sausage. Sarasota's best German market. Lots of smoked meats and deli items.

Morton's Gourmet Market • 1924 S. Osprey Ave. • 955-9856
WHAT YOU CAN FIND THERE: Upscale gourmet food items including a large selection of cheeses and wine. Great deli & carryout.

Morton's Siesta Market • 205 Canal Rd. • 349-1474
WHAT YOU CAN FIND THERE: Everyday grocery items plus a good selection of prepared foods for lunch and dinner. Cold beer.

Piccolo Italian Market • 6518 Gateway Ave. • 923-2202
WHAT YOU CAN FIND THERE: Italian market. Pastas, sauces, homebaked bread, and homemade Italian sausage. Sandwiches.

Southern Steer Butcher • 4084 Bee Ridge Rd. • 706-2625
WHAT YOU CAN FIND THERE: Big selection of pre-brined beef and chicken. Full butcher shop and lots of specialty items.

Walt's Fish Market • 4144 S. Tamiami Trl. • 921-4605
WHAT YOU CAN FIND THERE: Huge selection of fresh local fish & seafood. Stone crabs when in season. Smoked mullet spread!

MADFISH GRILL
4059 Cattleman Road
941-377-3474
madfishgrill.com

	SEAFOOD	COST: $$

HOURS: Mon-Sat, 11:30AM to 9PM • Sun, 11AM to 8PM
Sunday Brunch, 11AM to 2PM

WHAT TO EXPECT: Good For Families • Daily Specials
Happy Hour Bites Menu • Sunday Brunch Menu

BEST BITES: Chicken Cobb Salad • Bang Shrimp Bowl
Drunken Lobster Bisque • Blackened Grouper Sandwich
Tacos • Pan Seared Cod • Abuela's House-made Flan

SCAN FOR MENU

SOME BASICS
Reservations:	YES
Spirits:	FULL BAR
Parking:	LOT
Outdoor Dining:	YES

MADISON AVENUE DELI

28 North Boulevard of the Presidents
941-388-3354
madisondelisrq.com

ST ARMANDS	DELI	COST: $$

HOURS: Daily, 7:30AM to 4PM

WHAT TO EXPECT: Casual Dining • Nice Outdoor Dining Space
Breakfast & Lunch Only • Busy During Season

BEST BITES: California Chicken Salad • Reuben • Asian Chicken Wrap
Buffalo Chicken Panini • Roast Beef Salad • Cobb Salad
Breakfast Burrito • French Toast • Lox & Bagel

SCAN FOR MENU

SOME BASICS

Reservations:	NO
Spirits:	BEER/WINE
Parking:	LOT/STREET
Outdoor Dining:	YES

MAIN BAR SANDWICH SHOP

1944 Main Street
941-955-8733
themainbar.com

DOWNTOWN	DELI	COST: $

HOURS: Mon-Sat, 10AM to 4PM
CLOSED SUNDAY

WHAT TO EXPECT: Great For Quick Lunch • Easy On The Wallet
Lively Atmosphere • Fantastic Service

BEST BITES: Famous Italian Sandwich • New Yorker Sandwich
Homemade Soups • Tuna Salad Plate • Sultan Salad
Sarasotan Wrap • Key Lime Pie

SCAN FOR MENU

SOME BASICS

Reservations:	NO
Spirits:	BEER/WINE
Parking:	STREET
Outdoor Dining:	NO

MAISON BLANCHE

2605 Gulf of Mexico Drive (Four Winds Beach Resort)
941-383-8088
themaisonblanche.com

LONGBOAT KEY	FRENCH	COST: $$$$

HOURS: Wed-Sun, 5:30PM to 9:30PM •
CLOSED MONDAY & TUESDAY

WHAT TO EXPECT: Date Night! • Special Occasions
Excellent Service • Great Wine List • Online Reservations

BEST BITES: Wild Mushrooms Raviolis With Foie Gras Sauce
Chanterelles Risotto • Tomato Tart • Red Snapper
Beef Short Ribs • Chocolate Souffle With Creme Anglaise

SOME BASICS

SCAN FOR MENU

Reservations:	YES
Spirits:	BEER/WINE
Parking:	LOT
Outdoor Dining:	NO

MAR VISTA DOCKSIDE RESTAURANT & PUB

760 Broadway Street
941-383-2391
marvistadining.com

LONGBOAT KEY	AMERICAN	COST: $$

HOURS: Sun-Thur, 11:30AM to 9PM
Fri & Sat, 11:30AM to 10PM

WHAT TO EXPECT: Great For Families • Big List Of Specialty Drinks
Water View • Old Florida Feel • 14 Private Slips For Boaters

BEST BITES: Fish Dip • Beer & Old Bay Shrimp • Crab Cake Trio
Seafood Gumbo • Cobia Burger • Seafood Paella
Chef's Boil Pot • Coconut Cake

SOME BASICS

SCAN FOR MENU

Reservations:	NO
Spirits:	FULL BAR
Parking:	LOT
Outdoor Dining:	YES

MARCELLO'S RISTORANTE

4155 South Tamiami Trail
941-921-6794
marcellosarasota.com

SOUTH TRAIL	ITALIAN	COST: $$$

HOURS: Tue-Sat, 5:30PM to 9PM
CLOSED SUNDAY & MONDAY

WHAT TO EXPECT: Nice Wine List • Chef Driven Italian Cuisine
Small & Intimate Dining Experience

BEST BITES: Grilled Octopus • Beef Carpaccio • Lamb Ragu
Braised Beef Short Ribs • Diver Sea Scallops
Hudson Valley Duck Breast • Tiramisu • Cannoli

SCAN FOR INFO

SOME BASICS

Reservations:	YES
Spirits:	BEER/WINE
Parking:	LOT
Outdoor Dining:	NO

MARINA JACK'S

2 Marina Plaza
941-365-4232
marinajacks.com

DOWNTOWN	SEAFOOD	COST: $$$

HOURS: Sun-Thur, 11AM to 9PM
Fri & Sat, 11AM to 10PM

WHAT TO EXPECT: Water View • Dinner Cruises • Live Music
Nice Wine List • Live Music • Outdoor Lounge

BEST BITES: Filet Mignon Center Cut • Prawn Martini
Charcuterie Board • Sherry Crab Bisque • Mahi Francaise
Pan Seared Scallops • Bouillabaisse • Lump Crab Cakes

SCAN FOR MENU

SOME BASICS

Reservations:	YES
Spirits:	FULL BAR
Parking:	VALET/LOT
Outdoor Dining:	YES

MATTISON'S CITY GRILLE

1 North Lemon Avenue
941-330-0440
mattisons.com

DOWNTOWN	AMERICAN	COST: $$

HOURS: Lunch - Daily, 11AM to 3PM
Dinner - Daily, 4:30PM to 10PM

WHAT TO EXPECT: Great For A Date • Downtown Meet-Up Spot
Live Music • Great Bar Service • Happy Hour Daily

BEST BITES: Tuna Poke Tower • NE Clam Chowder • Shakshuka
Niman Ranch Reuben • Brick Oven Pizza!
Seafood Gumbo • Grouper Piccata • Key Lime Pie

SOME BASICS

SCAN FOR MENU

Reservations:	YES
Spirits:	FULL BAR
Parking:	STREET
Outdoor Dining:	YES

MATTISON'S FORTY ONE

7275 South Tamiami Trail
941-921-3400
mattisons.com

SOUTH TRAIL	AMERICAN	COST: $$

HOURS: Mon-Thur, 11:30AM to 9PM • Fri, 11:30AM to 10PM
Sat, 4:30PM to 10PM • CLOSED SUNDAY

WHAT TO EXPECT: Large Wine List • Brunch • Good Value
Online Reservations • Happy Hour Menu

BEST BITES: Artichokes Esther-Style • Wedge Salad • Pork Belly
Forty-One Burger • Rack Of Lamb • Fish & Chips
Maple Leaf Farms Duck • Thai Soba Noodle Bowl

SOME BASICS

SCAN FOR MENU

Reservations:	YES
Spirits:	FULL BAR
Parking:	LOT
Outdoor Dining:	NO

MEDITERRANEO

1970 Main Street
941-365-4122
mediterraneorest.com

DOWNTOWN	ITALIAN	COST: $$

HOURS: Lunch, Mon-Fri, 11:30AM to 2:30PM
Dinner, Daily from 5:30PM

WHAT TO EXPECT: Pizza • Good Wine List • Italian Specialties
Online Reservations • Private Party Dining Space

BEST BITES: Carpaccio Rucola • Mista Salad • Gamberi Salad
Minestrone Soup • Linguine Mare • Pollo Milanese
Paninis • Le Pizze Classiche • Profiteroles

SCAN FOR MENU

SOME BASICS

Reservations:	YES
Spirits:	FULL BAR
Parking:	STREET/GARAGE
Outdoor Dining:	YES

MELANGE

1568 Main Street
941-953-7111
melangesarasota.com

DOWNTOWN	AMERICAN	COST: $$$

HOURS: Wed-Sun, 5:30PM-10PM
CLOSED MONDAY & TUESDAY

WHAT TO EXPECT: Great For A Date • Adult Dining Experience
Open Late Night • Sophisticated Menu Options

BEST BITES: Baked Brie Salad • Cheese Board • Rabbit Tacos
Beef Short Ribs • Duck Brie Crepes • Stuffed Quail
Venison Osso Bucco • Bread Pudding

SCAN FOR MENU

SOME BASICS

Reservations:	YES
Spirits:	FULL BAR
Parking:	STREET
Outdoor Dining:	YES

MELIORA

1920 Hillview Street
941-444-7692
meliorarestaurant.com

SOUTHSIDE VILLAGE	AMERICAN	COST: $$$$

HOURS: Tues-Sat, 5PM to 9PM
CLOSED SUNDAY & MONDAY

WHAT TO EXPECT: Very Upscale Dining • Creative "Chef Driven" Menu
Reservations A Must • Chef's Table Seating Available

BEST BITES: Cold Menu Items - Raw Scallop, Cold Pork, Cucumber
Hot Menu Items - Fried Potato, Scamp Grouper, Gnocchi
Dessert Items - Japanese Cheesecake, Tomato Sorbet

SOME BASICS

SCAN FOR MENU

Reservations:	YES
Spirits:	FULL BAR
Parking:	STREET
Outdoor Dining:	NO

MICHAEL JOHN'S RESTAURANT

1040 Carlton Arms Boulevard
941-747-8032
michaeljohnsrestaurant.com

BRADENTON	FRENCH-AMERICAN	COST: $$$$

HOURS: Mon-Thur, 5PM to 9PM
Fri & Sat, 5PM to 10PM • CLOSED SUNDAY

WHAT TO EXPECT: American "Brasserie" • Upscale Dining Room
Great For A Special Occasion • Online Reservations

BEST BITES: Filet Paillards • Herbs de Provence • French Onion Soup
Baked French Escargot • The "Dirty" Caesar
Delmonico Ribeye • Raspberry and Port Wine Glazed Duck

SOME BASICS

SCAN FOR MENU

Reservations:	YES
Spirits:	FULL BAR
Parking:	LOT
Outdoor Dining:	NO

MICHAEL'S ON EAST

1212 East Avenue South
941-366-0007
bestfood.com

MIDTOWN PLAZA	AMERICAN	COST: $$$

HOURS: Tue-Thur, 5PM to 8:30PM • Fri & Sat, 5PM to 9PM
CLOSED SUNDAY AND MONDAY

WHAT TO EXPECT: Piano Lounge • Catering • Fine Dining
Opentable Reservations • AAA Four Diamond Award

BEST BITES: Lobster & Escargots • Mussels Marinière
East Avenue Caesar • Colony Snapper • Duck Two-Ways
Michael's Famous Bowtie Pasta • Brownie Ice Cream Stack

SCAN FOR MENU

SOME BASICS

Reservations:	YES
Spirits:	FULL BAR
Parking:	VALET
Outdoor Dining:	YES

MICHELLE'S BROWN BAG CAFÉ

1819 Main Street (City Center Building)
941-365-5858
michellesbrownbagcafe.com

DOWNTOWN	DELI	COST: $

HOURS: Mon-Fri, 9AM to 2PM
CLOSED SATURDAY & SUNDAY

WHAT TO EXPECT: Quick Lunch • Easy On The Wallet
Great Meet-Up Spot • Super Casual

BEST BITES: Longboat Brie Sandwich • Bayfront Tuna Sandwich
Farmer's Market Salad • Paninis • Lox & Bagel
Turkey Reuben • Half Sandwich + Soup!

SCAN FOR MENU

SOME BASICS

Reservations:	NO
Spirits:	BEER/WINE
Parking:	GARAGE/STREET
Outdoor Dining:	NO

MIGUEL'S

6631 Midnight Pass Road
941-349-4024
miguelsrestaurant.net

SIESTA KEY	FRENCH	COST: $$$

HOURS: Dinner, Daily from 4PM
Early Dinner Menu, 4PM to 6PM

WHAT TO EXPECT: Good Wine List • Quiet Atmosphere
Good Early Dining Menu • Nice For A Date

BEST BITES: Les Escargot Bourgogne • Steak Tartare
Sopa De Ajo • Les Fruits De Mer • Moules Normandy
Le Chateaubriand Bouquetiere • Le Veau Piccata

SOME BASICS

Reservations:	YES
Spirits:	FULL BAR
Parking:	LOT
Outdoor Dining:	NO

SCAN FOR MENU

MOLLY'S RESTAURANT & PUB

NEW

1562 Main Street
941-366-7711
eviesonline.com/location/mollys-pub

DOWNTOWN	IRISH	COST: $$

HOURS: Tues-Sat, 4PM to 10PM
CLOSED SUNDAY & MONDAY

WHAT TO EXPECT: Fun Pub Atmosphere • Downtown Location
Special Events • Great After Work Meetup Spot

BEST BITES: Shepherd's Pie • Bangers & Mash • Reuben
Cobb Salad • Hot Ham & Cheese • Deviled Eggs
Salmon BLT • Molly's Burger • Grilled Wings

SOME BASICS

Reservations:	NO
Spirits:	FULL BAR
Parking:	STREET/GARAGE
Outdoor Dining:	YES

SCAN FOR MENU

Make it at HOME

Bruschetta with Lemon Aioli and Herb Oil

Chef Martin Orozco-Ramirez
Duvals Fresh, Local, Seafood

INGREDIENTS - LEMON AIOLI
½ lemon
1 cup mayonnaise
1 dash Tabasco
1 pinch kosher salt
1/8 oz cilantro
¼ oz jalapenos
pinch of blackening seasoning
1/8 oz mustard
Pinch, black pepper

METHOD - LEMON AIOLI
Cut the seeds and stem from the jalapeno and add to blender.
Add remaining ingredients except for mayonnaise to the blender
and puree until smooth. Add the puree and mayo to a mixing
bowl and mix thoroughly until evenly combined.

INGREDIENTS - HERB OIL
½ oz parsley
1 small clove of garlic
pinch of black pepper
¼ oz fresh basil
1 pinch of salt
4 oz vegetable oil

METHOD - LEMON AIOLI
Combine all ingredients in blender and puree until smooth.

INGREDIENTS - BRUSCHETTA

1 medium shrimp (16/20)
1 dash of Tabasco
½ oz red onion
½ oz Roma tomato
1 very light pinch of kosher salt
½ oz Euro cucumber
1 oz fresh lime juice
1 oz fresh fish
3 baguette slices, ½" thick

METHOD - BRUSCHETTA

Dice your shrimp, onions, Roma tomatoes, cucumber, and fish into a quarter inch dice.

Combine with the lime juice, Tabasco, and salt, and gently hand mix.

Let rest for 1 hour. Seafood should become opaque.

Toast your baguette slices to the desired crispness. Spread a thin layer of aioli on the toasted crostini once cooled. Spoon equal portions of bruschetta mix on to each crostini and top with a light drizzle of herb oil. Enjoy!

Our menu was created by our local team of chefs and managers, taking inspiration from our beautiful home of Sarasota, Florida, and its unique culture. We feature a variety of innovative seafood and non-seafood dishes that are artfully and thoughtfully created and showcase the vast range of flavors of both land and sea. Together with our unique menu, our focus on excellent service allows us to deliver a one-of-a-kind dining experience in downtown Sarasota. Every menu item is prepared to order to allow for customization and personalization of each dish and to ensure you are getting the freshest possible meal. Our goal is to ensure we meet or exceed every guest's expectation. Whether you are celebrating a special occasion, visiting from out of town, or are a Sarasota local, we will do everything we can to ensure you leave satisfied. The restaurant is located at 1435 Main Street in Downtown Sarasota. Reservations at (941) 312-4001 or visit us on the web at duvalsfreshlocalseafood.com.

MONK'S STEAMER BAR

6690 Superior Avenue
941-927-3388
monkssteamerbar.com

GULF GATE	SEAFOOD	COST: $$

HOURS: Mon-Thur, 3PM to 12AM • Fri & Sat, 12PM to 1AM
Sunday, 12PM to 12AM

WHAT TO EXPECT: Steamed Everything! • Dive Bar/Great Food
Locals Favorite • Late Night Menu

BEST BITES: Seafood Bisque • Oysters Monkafeller • Mussels
Cajun Crawfish • Peel N Eat Shrimp • Oyster Shooters!

SCAN FOR MENU

SOME BASICS

Reservations:	NO
Spirits:	FULL BAR
Parking:	STREET/LOT
Outdoor Dining:	NO

MUNCHIES 420 CAFÉ

6639 Superior Avenue
941-929-9893
munchies420cafe.com

GULF GATE	AMERICAN	COST: $$

HOURS: Sun-Thur, 12PM to 3AM • Fri & Sat, 12PM to 4:20AM
Happy Hour, Daily, 12PM to 7PM

WHAT TO EXPECT: Crazy Sandwiches! • Super Laid Back • Late Night
Local Favorite

BEST BITES: MENU

SCAN FOR MENU

SOME BASICS

Reservations:	NO
Spirits:	FULL BAR
Parking:	LOT
Outdoor Dining:	YES

99 BOTTLES TAPROOM

1445 Second Street
941-487-7874
99bottles.net

DOWNTOWN	BEER	COST: $$

HOURS: Mon-Thur, 3PM to 11PM
Fri-Sun, 9AM to 12AM

WHAT TO EXPECT: Big City Feel • Knowledgeable Bar Staff
Small Menu Of Good Food • Great For An After Work Beer

BEST BITES: NY Bagel Brunch (Fri, Sat & Sun)
Pop Up Kitchens (Thur, Fri, Sat & Sun)

SOME BASICS

SCAN FOR MENU

Reservations:	NO
Spirits:	BEER/WINE
Parking:	STREET/GARAGE
Outdoor Dining:	YES

NANCY'S BAR-B-QUE

14475 State Road 70 E
941-999-2390
nancysbarbq.com

LWR	BBQ	COST: $

HOURS: Mon-Thur, 11AM to 9PM • Fri & Sat, 11AM to 10PM
Sunday, 11AM to 8OM

WHAT TO EXPECT: Casual Dining • Good For Families
Catering Available • Combo Meals • Great Pulled Pork!

BEST BITES: Pulled Pork & Chicken • Beef Brisket • Ribs
Combo Trays (Texas Holy Trinity) • Smoked Sausage
Brisket "Interstate Cheesesteak" • Baked Mac N Cheese

SOME BASICS

SCAN FOR MENU

Reservations:	NO
Spirits:	FULLBAR
Parking:	LOT
Outdoor Dining:	YES

SARASOTA
UPSCALE CHAIN DINING

Sarasota has a ton of great independently owned and operated restaurants. And, that's mostly what this dining book is all about. But, as with any decent sized city, we've got our share of quality, upscale chain dining options, too.

We've taken the time to put together a list of some of our favorites. Just like the main section of the book, we didn't have the space to list them all. So, we curated a collection of the ones we think will give you a consistent and favorable dining experience.

We've tried to include a little bit of everything here for you. Some steakhouses, sushi, deli, and even pizza. You'll recognize most of the names, I'm sure. There's something here for everyone.

Bonefish Grill • 3971 S. Tamiami Trl. • 924-9090
WHAT TO EXPECT: Upscale casual place to meet up with friends and enjoy drinks or dinner. Lots of seafood options. ($$)

Brio Tuscan Grille • 190 University Town Center Dr. • 702-9102
WHAT TO EXPECT: Italian cuisine. UTC. Online reservations. Lively atmosphere. Good for groups. ($$$)

Cooper's Hawk • 3130 Fruitville Commons Blvd. • 263-8100
WHAT TO EXPECT: Steaks, seafood, much more. Fantastic wine selection. Modern, casual dining. ($$$)

Capital Grille • 180 University Town Center Dr. • 256-3647
WHAT TO EXPECT: Big city steakhouse. Very upscale dining experience. Reservations/OpenTable. Private dining. ($$$$)

Chart House • 201 Gulf of Mexico Dr. • 383-5593
WHAT TO EXPECT: Fresh seafood. Nice gulf view. Always outstanding service. Classic upscale dining experience. ($$$)

Cheesecake Factory • 130 University Town Center Dr. • 256-3760
WHAT TO EXPECT: 200+ menu choices. Super large portions.
Happy Hour. Catering. Very busy dining atmosphere. ($$$)

Fleming's Prime Steakhouse • 2001 Siesta Dr. • 358-9463
WHAT TO EXPECT: Super high quality steaks + service. Private
dining. "Fleming's 100" wines. Happy Hour. ($$$$)

Hyde Park Steakhouse • 35 S. Lemon Ave. • 366-7788
WHAT TO EXPECT: Busy downtown location. Valet parking. Popular
Happy Hour. "Early Nights" menu. Private dining. ($$$$)

Kona Grill • 150 University Town Center Dr. • 256-8050
WHAT TO EXPECT: Heavy Asian influence cuisine. Sushi. Lively
dining experience. UTC Mall. Online reservations. ($$)

P.F. Changs Bistro • 766 S. Osprey Ave. • 296-6002
WHAT TO EXPECT: "Farm to Wok" Asian cuisine. Large menu. Busy,
vibrant atmosphere. Good for groups. Online reservations. ($$$)

Rodizio Brazilian Steakhouse • 5911 Fruitville Rd. • 260-8445
WHAT TO EXPECT: Brazilian steakhouse experience. Rotisserie
grilled meats. Tableside service. Large gourmet salad bar. ($$$)

Ruth's Chris Steakhouse • 6700 S. Tamiami Trl. • 942-8982
WHAT TO EXPECT: Exceptional service. Older dining crowd. Large
selection of USDA prime steaks. Great wine list. ($$$$)

Seasons 52 • 170 University Town Center Dr. • 702-5652
WHAT TO EXPECT: Seasonal menu selections. 52 wines by the
glass. UTC Mall. Group dining options. Great service. ($$$)

Sophie's • 120 University Town Center Dr. • 444-3077
WHAT TO EXPECT: UTC inside Saks FIfth Avenue. "Ladies" lunch
spot. Intimate dining experience. Great for private parties. ($$$)

NAPULÈ RISTORANTE ITALIANO

7129 South Tamiami Trail
941-556-9639
napulesarasota.com

SOUTH TRAIL	ITALIAN	COST: $$$

HOURS: Mon-Thur, 11:30AM to 9:30PM
Fri & Sat, 11:30AM to 10:30PM • CLOSED SUNDAY

WHAT TO EXPECT: Upscale Italian Dining • Great Wood Oven Pizza
Very Busy In Season • Vibrant Atmosphere

BEST BITES: Salumeria • Burrata • Bufala Salad • Fresella Salad
Trio di Bruschette • Polipetti Alla Luciana
Saltimbocca Di Vitello Alla Romana • Pizza!

SCAN FOR MENU

SOME BASICS

Reservations:	YES
Spirits:	FULL BAR
Parking:	LOT
Outdoor Dining:	YES

NELLIE'S DELI

15 South Beneva Road
941-924-2705
nelliescatering.com

	DELI	COST: $$

HOURS: Mon-Fri, 7AM to 2:30PM • Sat, 8AM to 2:30PM
CLOSED SUNDAY

WHAT TO EXPECT: Deli & Market • Great Catering Options
Casual Dining • Good For Families • Box Lunches!

BEST BITES: Lox & Bagel • Greek Breakfast Wrap • Fresh Fruit
Reuben Sandwiches • Italian Sub • Super BLT
Turkey Chef Salad • Homemade Soups • Quiche

SCAN FOR MENU

SOME BASICS

Reservations:	NO
Spirits:	NONE
Parking:	LOT
Outdoor Dining:	NO

NEW PASS GRILL & BAIT SHOP

1505 Ken Thompson Parkway
941-388-3050
newpassgrill.com

CITY ISLAND	AMERICAN	COST: $

HOURS: Daily, 7AM to 7PM

WHAT TO EXPECT: Casual Dining • Water View • More Than Burgers
Bait & Tackle Shop • A "Landmark" Since 1929

BEST BITES: Breakfast! • NE Clam Chowder • BLT
Hot Dog or Polish Sausage • New Pass Burgers
Fried Chicken Sandwich • Fish N Chips • Ice Cream Bar!

SOME BASICS

SCAN FOR MENU

Reservations:	NO
Spirits:	BEER/WINE
Parking:	LOT
Outdoor Dining:	YES

NICKY'S ON PALM

49 South Palm Avenue
941-330-1727
nickysbarandrestaurant.com

DOWNTOWN	AMERICAN	COST: $$$

HOURS: Wed, 6PM to 10PM • Thur, 6PM to 12AM • Fri, 6AM to 1AM
CLOSED SUNDAY, MONDAY & TUESDAY

WHAT TO EXPECT: Classic "Hollywood" Style • Piano Bar
Downtown Miromar Building Location

BEST BITES: Lobster Bisque • Escargots • Fried Calamari
Flatbreads • Lobster & Jumbo Shrimp Ravioli
Filet Mignon • Flan Caramel • Key Lime Pie

SOME BASICS

SCAN FOR MENU

Reservations:	YES
Spirits:	FULL BAR
Parking:	STREET
Outdoor Dining:	NO

Make it at
HOME

The Drum Circle

The Summer House Steak and Seafood Shark Tooth Vodka

INGREDIENTS
2 Oz Shark Tooth Premium Vodka
1 Oz fresh lime juice
1 Oz charred pineapple simple syrup

METHOD
Shake with ice and strain into your favorite cocktail glass with ice. Garnish with a fresh pineapple wedge.

THE SUMMER HOUSE STEAK AND SEAFOOD - Nestled in the heart of Siesta Key Village is a resort casual dining experience with impeccable service, delectable dishes, award winning wine list, and innovative craft cocktails. The owners of The Siesta Key Summer House Steak and Seafood Restaurant are committed to growing the hospitality and flavors of the key while continuing to preserve the natural beauty and uniqueness of our island. We pay homage to our Siesta Key Drum Circle and, in partnership with Shark Tooth Vodka of Venice, Florida, with our refreshing cocktail...

SHARK TOOTH VODKA - Life in Venice, Florida is the inspiration behind Shark Tooth Vodka. Bea Dale, a Polish / US citizen and Venice, Florida resident, wanted to capture the essence of life in Venice in a way that everyone could enjoy. Since its release in 2021, Shark Tooth Vodka has rapidly become a Florida favorite. Its smooth start and sweet finish are trademark flavors created by blending Florida sweet corn, pure water from the aquifer, and an exclusive recipe of cultured fermenting yeasts. The Shark Tooth Necklace on every bottle is our gift, assuring you that you're getting authentic Shark Tooth Vodka. 100% Natural. 100% Florida.

OAK & STONE

5405 University Parkway*
941-225-4590
oakandstone.com

UPARK	AMERICAN	COST: $$

HOURS: Sun-Thur, 11AM to 10PM
Fri & Sat, 11AM to 12AM

WHAT TO EXPECT: Great For Sports Viewing • Lively Atmosphere
Live Music • Large Beer Selection • Pizza Too!

BEST BITES: Philly Cheesesteak Egg Rolls • Beer Cheese Soup
Buffalo Chicken Bowl • Pizza! • Crispy Grouper BLT
Classic Reuben • Griddle Burger

SOME BASICS

SCAN FOR MENU

Reservations: NO
Spirits: FULL BAR
Parking: LOT
Outdoor Dining: YES

OASIS CAFÉ & BAKERY

3542 South Osprey Avenue
941-957-1214
theoasiscafe.net

	AMERICAN	COST: $$

HOURS: Tue-Fri, 7AM to 2PM • Sat & Sun, 8AM to 1:30PM
CLOSED MONDAY

WHAT TO EXPECT: Breakfast & Lunch • Casual Dining
Great Daily Specials • Homemade Pastries & Baked Goods

BEST BITES: Eggs Benedict • Cheese Blintzes • Lox & Bagel
Italian Scramble • Blackened Basa Reuben
Soup & Salad Combo • Siesta Sister Wrap

SOME BASICS

SCAN FOR MENU

Reservations: NO
Spirits: BEER/WINE
Parking: LOT
Outdoor Dining: YES

THE OLD SALTY DOG

5023 Ocean Boulevard*
941-349-0158
theoldsaltydog.com

SIESTA KEY	AMERICAN	COST: $$

HOURS: Daily, 11AM to 9PM

WHAT TO EXPECT: Locals Love It • Vacation Feel • Cold Beer
As Seen On TV! • Great For Families • Friendly Bar Staff

BEST BITES: Hand-Cut Onion Rings • Peel N Eat Shrimp
NE Clam Chowder • The Famous "Salty Dog"
Grouper Reuben • Firecracker Wrap • Fish 'N Chips

SCAN FOR MENU

SOME BASICS

Reservations:	NO
Spirits:	FULL BAR
Parking:	STREET
Outdoor Dining:	YES

O'LEARY'S TIKI BAR & GRILL

5 Bayfront Drive
941-953-7505
olearystikibar.com

DOWNTOWN	AMERICAN	COST: $$

HOURS: Sun-Thur, 8AM to 10PM
Fri & Sat, 8AM to 11PM

WHAT TO EXPECT: Live Music • Beach Bar • Cold Beer
Great Views • Watersports Rentals • Super Relaxed

BEST BITES: Mozzarella Sticks • Peel & Eat Shrimp
Rachel Sandwich • Soft Shell Crab Sandwich • Mahi Tacos
The Works Burger • Ultimate Margarita

SCAN FOR MENU

SOME BASICS

Reservations:	NO
Spirits:	FULL BAR
Parking:	LOT
Outdoor Dining:	YES

OPHELIA'S ON THE BAY

9105 Midnight Pass Road
941-349-2212
opheliasonthebay.net

SIESTA KEY	AMERICAN	COST: $$$

HOURS: Dinner Nightly, 5PM to 10PM

WHAT TO EXPECT: Great For A Date • Nice Water View
Good Wine List • Opentable Reservations

BEST BITES: Thai Oishii Shrimp Cocktail • Escargot Ophelia
Vermont Creamery Chevre & Chioggia Beets
Key West Yellowtail Snapper • Thomas Farms Rack Of Lamb

SOME BASICS

SCAN FOR MENU

Reservations:	YES
Spirits:	FULL BAR
Parking:	VALET
Outdoor Dining:	YES

OPUS RESTAURANT & LOUNGE

`NEW`

6644 Gateway Avenue
941-925-2313
opus-srq.com

GULF GATE	AMERICAN	COST: $$$

HOURS: Tues-Fri, 11:30AM to 9PM • Sat, 3PM to 10PM
CLOSED SUNDAY & MONDAY

WHAT TO EXPECT: Upscale Dining Experience • Private Dining Space
Great Outdoor Dining Area • Lots Of Parking

BEST BITES: Spanish Mussels • 48 Hour Frites • Lamb Chops
Nicoise Salad • Confit Pork Shank • Cioppino
Olive Oil Chocolate Zucchini Cake

SOME BASICS

SCAN FOR MENU

Reservations:	YES
Spirits:	FULL BAR
Parking:	LOT/STREET
Outdoor Dining:	YES

ORIGIN CRAFT BEER & PIZZA CAFÉ

1837 Hillview Street*
941-316-9222
originpizzacafe.com

SOUTHSIDE VILLAGE	PIZZA	COST: $$

HOURS: Sun-Thur, 11AM to 1AM
Fri & Sat, 11AM to 2AM

WHAT TO EXPECT: Neighborhood Feel • Open Late • Friendly Staff
Local Favorite • 4 Sarasota Area Locations • Craft Beer

BEST BITES: Great Wings! • Pizza! • Quinoa Tab'bouleh Salad
Stromboli • Mediterranean Platter • Meatballs

SCAN FOR MENU

SOME BASICS
Reservations:	NO
Spirits:	BEER/WINE
Parking:	LOT/STREET
Outdoor Dining:	YES

ORTYGIA

1418 13th Street W.
941-741-8646
ortygiarestaurant.com

BRADENTON	EUROPEAN	COST: $$$

HOURS: Wed-Sat, 5PM to 8PM
CLOSED SUNDAY, MONDAY & TUESDAY

WHAT TO EXPECT: Intimate Dining Experience • Chef Driven Menu
Nice Outdoor Dining Space • Village Of The Arts

BEST BITES: Mushroom Pate • Veal Piccata • Timballo
"Seafood Of The Week" • Dark Chocolate Pate
Pasta La Norma • Locally Made Gelato

SCAN FOR MENU

SOME BASICS
Reservations:	YES
Spirits:	BEER/WINE
Parking:	STREET
Outdoor Dining:	YES

OWEN'S FISH CAMP

516 Burns Court
941-951-6936
owensfishcamp.com

BURNS COURT	**SEAFOOD**	**COST: $$**

HOURS: Daily, 4PM to 9PM

WHAT TO EXPECT: Fun Dining Experience • Good For Families
Busy In Season • Parking Can Be A Challenge

BEST BITES: Deviled Eggs • Garlic Snail With Chorizo
Maryland Spiced Shrimp • Low Country Boil
Crispy Chicken • Spicy Jambalaya • Shrimp & Grits

SOME BASICS

SCAN FOR MENU

Reservations:	NO
Spirits:	FULL BAR
Parking:	STREET/LOT
Outdoor Dining:	YES

PACIFIC RIM

1859 Hillview Street
941-330-8071
pacrimsrq.com

SOUTHSIDE VILLAGE	**ASIAN**	**COST: $$**

HOURS: Mon-Fri, 11:30AM to 2PM • Mon-Thur, 4:30PM to 9PM
Fri & Sat, 4:30PM to 10PM • Sun, 4:30PM to 9PM

WHAT TO EXPECT: Fun Dining Experience • Sushi & More
Parking Usually Available • Happy Hour

BEST BITES: Crispy Spring Roll • Tuna Carpaccio • Sushi
Sashimi • Drunken Noodles • Wok Dishes • Red Curry
Teriyaki Chicken • Shrimp Tempura • Green Tea Ice Cream

SOME BASICS

SCAN FOR MENU

Reservations:	YES
Spirits:	FULL BAR
Parking:	LOT/STREET
Outdoor Dining:	YES

THE PARROT PATIO BAR & GRILL

3602 Webber Street
941-952-3352
theparrotpatiobar.com

AMERICAN	COST: $$

HOURS: Sun-Thur, 11:30AM to 11PM
Fri & Sat, 11AM to 12AM

WHAT TO EXPECT: Very Casual • Sports Bar Feel • Live Music
NFL Football Package • Good For Groups

BEST BITES: Smoked Fish Dip • Coconut Shrimp • Buffalo Wings
Buffalo Shrimp • Southwest Taco Salad • Seared Ahi Tuna
Pizza! • Beef On Weck • Grouper Reuben • Burgers

SCAN FOR MENU

SOME BASICS

Reservations:	NO
Spirits:	FULL BAR
Parking:	LOT
Outdoor Dining:	YES

PASTRY ART

1512 Main Street
941-955-7545
pastryartcafe.com

DOWNTOWN	AMERICAN	COST: $$

HOURS: Mon-Sat, 7AM to 4PM
Sun, 8AM to 3PM

WHAT TO EXPECT: Great For A Coffee Date • Wi-Fi
Busy Weekend Spot • Casual Downtown Hangout

BEST BITES: Avocado Toast • Lox & Bagel • Steak & Egg Sandwich
Reuben Sandwich • Beet Salad • Rainbow Salad
Turkey Avocado BLT • Homemade Soup

SCAN FOR MENU

SOME BASICS

Reservations:	NO
Spirits:	BEER/WINE
Parking:	STREET
Outdoor Dining:	YES

Food Trucks are popular. And, just like every other great food community, we've got our share roaming the streets. Here's a little basic info to help you navigate through the maze of local mobile dining options. These are a few of our favorites!

HAMLET'S EATERY
What They Serve: Tacos and slider boxes. Both meat and vegan options are available.
Where You Can Find Them:
The Bazaar on Apricot & Lime
Info at: hamletseatery.com

THE MAINE LINE
What They Serve: Lobster a bunch of different ways. Also Clam "Chowdah." Try a Lobstah Grilled Cheese!
Where You Can Find Them: Various locations around the Sarasota area. Check their website for details.
Info at: themaineline.net

MOUTHOLE BBQ
What They Serve: BBQ, BBQ, AND BBQ. Beef, pork, ribs, and chicken. Also a seriously great burger!
Where You Can Find Them: Various locations around the Sarasota area. Check their Facebook page for details.
Info at: moutholebbq.com

SIMPLY GREEK BY WYNNBERRY
What They Serve: Authentic Greek cuisine in a food truck! Gyros, moussaka and more. Try the Greek fries.
Where You Can Find Them:
Various stops around the Sarasota area.
Info at: simplygreekbywynnberry.com

PATRICK'S 1481

1481 Main Street
941-955-1481
patricks1481.com

DOWNTOWN	AMERICAN	COST: $$

HOURS: Mon-Thur, 11AM to 9PM • Fri, 11AM to 10PM
Sat, 10AM to 10PM • Sun, 10AM to 9PM

WHAT TO EXPECT: Downtown Since 1985 • Local Favorite
Good Craft Beer Selection • Known For Their Burgers

BEST BITES: Spinach & Artichoke Dip • Roasted Beet Salad
1481 Salad • Award Winning Burgers • Scampi
Fish N Chips • Yankee Pot Roast • Key Lime Pie

SCAN FOR MENU

SOME BASICS

Reservations:	YES
Spirits:	FULL BAR
Parking:	STREET/VALET
Outdoor Dining:	YES

PHILLIPPI CREEK OYSTER BAR

5353 South Tamiami Trail
941-925-4444
creekseafood.com

SOUTH TRAIL	SEAFOOD	COST: $$

HOURS: Daily 11AM to 9:30PM
Happy Hour, 3PM to 5:30PM

WHAT TO EXPECT: Great For Families • Water View • Casual Dining
Busy During Season • Good For Kids

BEST BITES: Oysters Rockefeller • Fried Smelt • Florida Cobb Salad
Jumbo Shrimp Cocktail • Oysters! • "Norfolks"
Steamed Pots • Seafood Paella • Root Beer Float

SCAN FOR MENU

SOME BASICS

Reservations:	NO
Spirits:	FULL BAR
Parking:	LOT
Outdoor Dining:	YES

PHO CALI

1578 Main Street
941-955-2683
phocalisarasota.com

DOWNTOWN	VIETNAMESE	COST: $

HOURS: Mon-Thur, 11AM to 9PM • Fri & Sat, 11AM to 9:30PM
CLOSED SUNDAY

WHAT TO EXPECT: Great Service • Casual Dining
Easy On The Wallet • Good For Families • Noodle Bowls!

BEST BITES: Pork & Shrimp Vietnamese Pancake • Roasted Quail
Daily Specials • Pho Noodle Bowls • Noodle Stir Fry
Rice Vermicelli Noodle Bowls • Roasted Duck

SOME BASICS

SCAN FOR MENU

Reservations:	NO
Spirits:	BEER/WINE
Parking:	STREET
Outdoor Dining:	NO

PICCOLO ITALIAN MARKET & DELI

6518 Gateway Avenue
941-923-2202
piccolomarket.com

GULF GATE	ITALIAN	COST: $

HOURS: Tue-Sat, 11AM to 5PM
CLOSED SUNDAY & MONDAY

WHAT TO EXPECT: Great For A Quick Lunch • Italian Market
Super Casual • Delicious Sandwiches • Catering Available

BEST BITES: Italian Chopped Salad • The Godfather Sandwich
Meatball Parm Sandwich • Pizza! • Pasta Marinara
Chicken Piccata • Cannoli

SOME BASICS

SCAN FOR MENU

Reservations:	NO
Spirits:	NONE
Parking:	LOT
Outdoor Dining:	NO

PIER 22

1200 1st Avenue West
941-748-8087
pier22dining.com

BRADENTON	SEAFOOD	COST: $$$

HOURS: Mon-Thur, 11:30AM to 10PM • Fri, 11:30AM to 10:30PM
Sat, 8AM to 10:30PM • Sun, 8AM to 10PM

WHAT TO EXPECT: Great For A Date • Water View • Good Wine List
Happy Hour • Weekend Brunch

BEST BITES: Asian Lettuce Wrap • Poutine • Fish Tacos
Flatbreads • NE Clam Chowder • Cobb Salad
Grouper Piccata • New York Cheesecake

SCAN FOR MENU

SOME BASICS

Reservations:	YES
Spirits:	FULL BAR
Parking:	LOT
Outdoor Dining:	YES

PIZZA N' BREW

1507 Main Street*
941-259-3894
pizzanbrew.com

DOWNTOWN	PIZZA	COST: $$

HOURS: Sun-Thur 11AM to 2AM
Fri & Sat, 11AM to 3AM

WHAT TO EXPECT: Late Night Spot • Casual Pizza And Beer
Downtown & Siesta Key Locations

BEST BITES: Garlic Cheese Bread • Classic Caesar Salad
Buffalo Wings • Meatball Sandwich • Calzone
Pizza! • Burgers • Chicken Parm Sandwich

SCAN FOR MENU

SOME BASICS

Reservations:	NO
Spirits:	BEER/WINE
Parking:	STREET
Outdoor Dining:	NO

THE POINT
131 Bayview Drive
941-786-3890
eviesonline.com/location/the-point

OSPREY	SEAFOOD	COST: $$

HOURS: Daily, 11AM to 10PM

WHAT TO EXPECT: Three Floors Of Dining • Great Gulf Views
Happy Hour Daily • Arrive By Boat! • Historic Spanish Point

BEST BITES: Mahi Mahi Bites • Bangin' Shrimp • Crab Cakes
Porterhouse Pork Chop • On Point Burger
Lobster Roll • Salmon BLT • Roasted Cauliflower

SOME BASICS
SCAN FOR MENU

Reservations:	YES
Spirits:	FULL BAR
Parking:	LOT
Outdoor Dining:	YES

POP'S SUNSET GRILL
112 Circuit Road (ICW Marker 10 by boat)
941-488-3177
popssunsetgrill.com

NOKOMIS	SEAFOOD	COST: $$

HOURS: Daily, 8AM to 10PM

WHAT TO EXPECT: Online "Waitlist" • Serving Breakfast!
Water View • Vacation Atmosphere • Great For Families

BEST BITES: Sunrise Benedict • Shrimp Cocktail • NE Clam Chowder
Pizza! • Raw Bar • Coconut Shrimp • Burgers
Grouper Reuben • Chocolate Toffee Mousse Cake

SOME BASICS
SCAN FOR MENU

Reservations:	NO
Spirits:	FULL BAR
Parking:	LOT
Outdoor Dining:	YES

Make it at HOME

Artichoke Caesar Dressing
Chef Chris Covelli, Sage

INGREDIENTS
1 quart mayonnaise
20 cloves garlic, roasted
15 anchovies
2 cups Parmesan cheese
12 ounces artichoke hearts

METHOD
Pre-heat oven to 350°. Wrap garlic tightly in aluminum foil. Roast until brown. Approximately 30-40 minutes.

Sear the artichoke hearts until golden brown.

In a food processor, pulse all ingredients except Parmesan until smooth. Then fold in the Parmesan slowly so as not to break the dressing.

Season to taste. Enjoy!

Located at 1216 First Street, Sage Restaurant brings a unique international culinary experience to its downtown location. Guests are treated to worldly cuisine with carefully curated and inspired cocktails. Sage's menu is seasonally inspired with ingredients and cooking styles from around the world. Award-winning Executive Chef Christopher Covelli's professional culinary career spans seven different countries, and he brings authenticity to every dish, creating the ultimate culinary experience for guests. His approach to the menu is similar to the building itself, with a strong sense of place and romance that creates a warm and inviting ambiance with rich character and attention to every detail.

PRIME SERIOUS STEAK

133 South Tamiami Trail
941-837-8325
primeserioussteak.com/newsite

VENICE	STEAKHOUSE	COST: $$$

HOURS: Mon-Sat, 4PM to 10PM
Sun, 12PM to 9PM

WHAT TO EXPECT: Steakhouse Atmosphere • Happy Hour Daily
2nd Location In Port Charlotte • Busy In Season

BEST BITES: Onion Brick • Shrimp Cocktail • Carpaccio
Prime Steakburger • Maple Bourbon Chicken
Filet Au Poivre • Prime Rib • New Zealand Lamb Chops

SOME BASICS

SCAN FOR MENU

Reservations:	YES
Spirits:	FULL BAR
Parking:	LOT
Outdoor Dining:	NO

REEF CAKES

1812 South Osprey Avenue
941-444-7968
reefcakes.com

SOUTHSIDE VILLAGE	SEAFOOD	COST: $$

HOURS: Tues-Fri, 11AM to 9PM • Sat, 3PM to 9PM
CLOSED SUNDAY & MONDAY

WHAT TO EXPECT: Fish Cakes • Casual Dining Experience

BEST BITES: Smoked Salmon Deviled Eggs • Adult Fish Sticks
Shrimp Cocktail • The Cod Father Sandwich
Fusion Salad • Key Lime Pie • Bread Pudding

SOME BASICS

SCAN FOR INFO

Reservations:	NO
Spirits:	BEER/WINE
Parking:	STREET
Outdoor Dining:	NO

REYNA'S TAQUERIA

935 North Beneva Road (Sarasota Commons)
941-260-8343
reynastaqueria.com

SARASOTA COMMONS	MEXICAN	COST: $

HOURS: Mon-Sat, 11AM to 9PM
Sun,11AM to 3PM

WHAT TO EXPECT: Family Friendly • Daily Specials
Lots Of Parking • Authentic Mexican Cuisine

BEST BITES: Birria Tacos • Burrito Bowls • Tortas • Sopas
Chips and Guacamole • Churros • Flan

SCAN FOR MENU

SOME BASICS

Reservations:	NO
Spirits:	BEER/WINE
Parking:	LOT
Outdoor Dining:	NO

RICK'S FRENCH BISTRO

2177 Siesta Drve
941-957-0533
ricksfrenchbistro.com

SOUTHGATE	FRENCH	COST: $$$

HOURS: Wed-Sat, 5PM to 9PM
CLOSED SUNDAY, MONDAY & TUESDAY

WHAT TO EXPECT: Initmate Dining Experience • Limited Seating
Authentic French Cuisine • Lots Of Parking

BEST BITES: Soupe a l'Oignon Gratinee • Saumon Fume Sur Toasts
Steak au Poivre • Crevettes a la Marseillaise
Boeuf Bourguignon • Chocolate Mousse

SCAN FOR MENU

SOME BASICS

Reservations:	YES
Spirits:	BEER/WINE
Parking:	LOT
Outdoor Dining:	NO

RIPFIRE PIZZA & BBQ
5218 Ocean Boulevard
941-313-7511
ripfirepizza.com

SIESTA KEY	PIZZA	COST: $$

HOURS: Daily, 11AM to 10PM

WHAT TO EXPECT: Fast Fired Pizza • In The Heart Of Siesta Village
Good Craft Beer Selection • Family Friendly

BEST BITES: Pizza! • BBQ Pork Platter • Caesar Salad
Mac N Cheese • Housemade Cider Vinegar Slaw

SOME BASICS

SCAN FOR MENU

Reservations:	NO
Spirits:	BEER/WINE
Parking:	STREET
Outdoor Dining:	YES

RIVERHOUSE REEF & GRILL
995 Riverside Drive
941-729-0616
riverhousefl.com

PALMETTO	SEAFOOD	COST: $$$

HOURS: Mon-Thur, 11:30AM to 9PM • Fri, 11:30AM to 10PM
Sat, 11AM to 10PM • Sun, 11AM to 9PM

WHAT TO EXPECT: Waterfront Dining • Happy Hour
Sunday Brunch • Regatta Pointe Marina

BEST BITES: Blue Crab Dip • Oysters • Island Time Salad
Lobster Corn Chowder • Grouper Tacos
Burgers • Lobster Roll • Lobster Pot Pie

SOME BASICS

SCAN FOR MENU

Reservations:	YES
Spirits:	FULL BAR
Parking:	LOT
Outdoor Dining:	YES

Craft beer, brew pubs, and full on local breweries. Sarasota is not immune to the small batch beer craze. As a matter of fact, we've got some damn good beer craftsmen right here in town. Oh, and along with these local artisans are some great places to down a few unique brews. Here's a list of some of our local favorites. - Cheers!

SARASOTA BREWERIES & BREWPUBS

BIG TOP BREWING
975 Cattlemen Road
Sarasota, FL 34232
941-371-2939
bigtopbrewing.com

BREW LIFE BREWING
5765 South Beneva Road
Sarasota, FL 34233
941-952-3831
brewlifebrewing.com

CALUSA BREWING
5377 McIntosh Road
Sarasota, FL 34233
941-922-8150
calusabrewing.com

GOOD LIQUID BREWING
1570 Lakefront Drive
Sarasota, FL 34240
941-238-6466
goodliquidbrewingcompany.com

MOTORWORKS BREWING
1014 9th Street W
Bradenton, FL 34205
941-567-6218
motorworksbrewing.com

SUN KIN BREWING
1215 Mango Avenue
Sarasota, FL 34237
941-893-3940
sunkingbrewing.com

SARASOTA BEER BARS

99 BOTTLES
1445 2nd Street
Sarasota, FL 34236
941-487-7874
99bottles.net

SHAMROCK PUB
2257 Ringling Boulevard
Sarasota, FL 34237
941-952-1730
shamrocksarasota.com

Please Drink Responsibly

RODIZIO GRILL

5911 Fruitville Road
941-260-8445
rodiziogrill.com/sarasota

BRAZILIAN	**COST: $$$**

HOURS: Mon-Thur, 5PM to 9PM • Fri, 5PM to 10PM
Sat, 12PM to 10PM • Sun, 12PM to 9PM

WHAT TO EXPECT: Brazilian Steakhouse • Fun For A Group
Big Salad Buffet • Lots Of Parking

BEST BITES: Maminha • Bife Com Alho • Galeto
Linguiça • Cordeiro • Crème Brûlée

SCAN FOR MENU

SOME BASICS

Reservations:	YES
Spirits:	FULL BAR
Parking:	LOT
Outdoor Dining:	NO

ROESSLER'S

2033 Vamo Way
941-966-5688
roesslersrestaurant.com

SOUTH TRAIL	**EUROPEAN**	**COST: $$$**

HOURS: Dinner, Tues-Sun, 5PM to close
CLOSED MONDAY

WHAT TO EXPECT: Good Wine List • Private Dining Room
Family Owned & Operated Since 1978 • Online Reservations

BEST BITES: Crispy Duckling New Orleans • Snapper Pontchartrain
Bouillabaisse • Wiener Schnitzel Holstein • Steak Diane
Vichyssois • The Wedge • Bananas Foster

SCAN FOR MENU

SOME BASICS

Reservations:	YES
Spirits:	FULL BAR
Parking:	LOT
Outdoor Dining:	YES

ROMANSQ

6670 Superior Avenue
941-237-8742
romansq.com

GULF GATE	PIZZA	COST: $$

HOURS: Wed-Sat, 12PM to 12AM • Sun, 11AM to 6PM
CLOSED MONDAY & TUESDAY

WHAT TO EXPECT: "Roman" Style Pizza • Fresh Baked Bread
Online Ordering

BEST BITES: Fra Diavolo Pizza • Genovese Pesto Pizza
Margherita Pizza • Salsiccia Fungi Pizza
Pizzas Comes In Two Sizes, Half & Full "Tray"

SOME BASICS

SCAN FOR MENU

Reservations:	NO
Spirits:	NONE
Parking:	LOT/STREET
Outdoor Dining:	NO

ROSEBUD'S STEAKHOUSE & SEAFOOD

2215 South Tamiami Trail
941-918-8771
rosebudssarasota.com

OSPREY	STEAKHOUSE	COST: $$$

HOURS: Tues-Sun, 4PM to 10PM
CLOSED MONDAY

WHAT TO EXPECT: Early Bird Dining • Private Dining Room
Aged, Hand Cut, Angus Steaks • Established 1995

BEST BITES: Oysters On The Half Shell • Escargot • Duck Wings
Prime Rib • Surf & Turf • Center Cut Pork Chops
BBQ Ribs • Sea Bass "Crab Louie" • Key Lime Pie

SOME BASICS

SCAN FOR MENU

Reservations:	YES
Spirits:	FULL BAR
Parking:	LOT
Outdoor Dining:	NO

THE ROSEMARY

411 North Orange Avenue
941-955-7600
therosemarysarasota.com

ROSEMARY DISTRICT	AMERICAN	COST: $$

HOURS: Tue-Fri, 11AM to 2PM
Sat, 9AM to 2PM

WHAT TO EXPECT: Casual Atmosphere • Busy In Season
Great Outdoor Dining Space • Nice Lunch Spot

BEST BITES: Buttermilk Pancakes • Quiche Lorraine
Omelets • Prix Fixe Lunch Menu • Bermuda Fish Chowder
Thai Chicken Salad • Red Snapper BLT

SCAN FOR MENU

SOME BASICS

Reservations:	YES
Spirits:	BEER/WINE
Parking:	STREET
Outdoor Dining:	YES

ROSEMARY AND THYME

511 North Orange Avenue
941-955-7600
therosemarysarasota.com

ROSEMARY DISTRICT	AMERICAN	COST: $$$

HOURS: Tue-Sun, 4:30PM to 9PM
Sunday Brunch, 9AM to 2PM

WHAT TO EXPECT: Upscale, But Casual • Fantastic Sunday Brunch
Great Appetizers • Don't Forget Dessert

BEST BITES: Belgian Waffle • Greek Quiche • Avocado Toast
Bermuda Fish Cake Benedict • Escargots
Pistachio-Dusted Salmon • Steak Frites

SCAN FOR INFO

SOME BASICS

Reservations:	YES
Spirits:	FULL BAR
Parking:	STREET
Outdoor Dining:	NO

SAGE

1216 First Street
941-445-5660
sagesrq.com

DOWNTOWN	AMERICAN	COST: $$$

HOURS: Tues-Thur, 5PM to 10PM
Fri & Sat, 5PM to 11PM

WHAT TO EXPECT: Upscale Dining • Private Event Space
Online Reservations • Rooftop Bar Is Great For A Date

BEST BITES: Seasonal Menu • Bison Short Rib • House Made Rigatoni
Portuguese Mussels • Maple Leak Farms Duck
Beyond S'Mores • Creme Brulee

SOME BASICS

Reservations:	YES
Spirits:	FULL BAR
Parking:	LOT/STREET
Outdoor Dining:	YES

SCAN FOR MENU

Scan for the latest Sarasota
Restaurant news.
Subscribe to our newsletter

sarasota bites

SARDINIA

5770 South Tamiami Trail
941-702-8582
sardiniasrq.com

SOUTH TRAIL	ITALIAN	COST: $$$

HOURS: Mon-Sat, 5PM to 10PM
CLOSED SUNDAY

WHAT TO EXPECT: Small & Intimate Dining • Homemade Dishes
Private Dining Room Available • Chef Driven Menu

BEST BITES: Antipasto • Carpaccio • Minestrone • Gnocchi
Lasagna • Ravioli Di Vitello Al Burro, Salvia, Noci E Pecorino
Spigola Al Sale • Chocolate Mousse • Warm Zabaione

SCAN FOR MENU

SOME BASICS

Reservations:	YES
Spirits:	BEER/WINE
Parking:	LOT
Outdoor Dining:	NO

SCHNITZEL KITCHEN

6521 Superior Avenue
941-922-9299
sites.google.com/view/schnitzelsrq/home

GULF GATE	GERMAN	COST: $$

HOURS: Tues-Sun, 4PM to 9PM
CLOSED SUNDAY & MONDAY

WHAT TO EXPECT: Casual Ethnic Cuisine • Homemade Dishes
Big German Beer Selection

BEST BITES: Kinder Sausage • Potato Pancakes • Schweinhaxe
Wiener Schnitzel • Chicken Paprika • Gulash
Schweinebraten • Spätzle • Apple Strudel

SCAN FOR MENU

SOME BASICS

Reservations:	YES
Spirits:	BEER & WINE
Parking:	LOT/STREET
Outdoor Dining:	NO

SCREAMING GOAT TAQUERIA

6566 Gateway Avenue
941-210-3992
screaming-goat.com

GULF GATE	MEXICAN	COST: $

HOURS: Mon-Sat, 11AM to 8PM
CLOSED SUNDAY

WHAT TO EXPECT: Super Casual • Taco Shack • Family Friendly
Great For A Quick Lunch Or Dinner • Private Event Space

BEST BITES: Tacos, Burritos & Bowls • Pork Cochinita Pibil
Latin Falafel • Pollo Asado • Beef Barbacoa
Vegan Chorizo • Chips & Guac

SOME BASICS

SCAN FOR MENU

Reservations:	NONE
Spirits:	BEER/WINE
Parking:	LOT/STREET
Outdoor Dining:	NO

SELVA GRILL

1345 Main Street*
941-362-4427
selvagrill.com

DOWNTOWN	PERUVIAN	COST: $$$

HOURS: Sun-Thur, 5PM to 11PM
Fri & Sat, 5PM to 1AM

WHAT TO EXPECT: Great For A Date • Great Ceviche
Late Night & Happy Hour Menus • Also A UTC Location

BEST BITES: Wahoo Ceviche • Selva Wild Ceviche • Tuna Tiradito
Empanadas • Selva's Crab Cake • Atun a la Parilla
Selva's Famous Skirt Steak • Malbec Braised Short Ribs

SOME BASICS

SCAN FOR MENU

Reservations:	YES
Spirits:	FULL BAR
Parking:	STREET/PALM GARAGE
Outdoor Dining:	YES

Your Pocket Wine
COMPANION

By Lorenzo Muslia, Partner - Andis Wines

Wine is a wonderful world that is hard to simplify into white or red. It is one of the oldest beverages in the world, dating back 5000 years.

In this short list, I have the pleasure of guiding you through a list of wine styles that are easy to find in your local restaurant and wine shop. I prefer to divide wine into five components that are very different from each other:

1) Body can be from light to full, which is how we perceive the wine on our palate.

2) Sweetness can vary from bone dry to sweet and is measured by the residual sugar (RS) found in wine.

3) Tannins is perceived as bitter in wine; the younger the wine is, the more tannins are in it; it also varies from variety to variety. A Pinot Noir has fewer tannins than Petite Sirah.

4) Acidity is what gives the wine a tart and sour taste. It varies from 3.1 for white wines (lemonade is 2.6)pH to just around 4.1 for red wines (coffee is 4.5)pH.

5) Alcohol can taste bitter, sweet, spicy, or oily in different stages. It is formed during fermentation as the yeast converts the sugars into ethanol and releases CO_2. In wine ranges from 5% to over 15%.

If one of these is very dominant and then we have a wine that is most likely off balance and will not be an easy food pairing, but once these components find a harmonious balance, great pleasure is achieved. Wines that are balanced between their components are easier to pair with food and provide a better taste.

REDS

Red wine is the largest selection of wine on the market, and here's a guide to the most famous varieties and their blends.

CABERNET SAUVIGNON, BORDEAUX BLEND, MERITAGE & BOLGHERI

Characteristics: Black Cherry, White Pepper, Cedar, Graphite, and Baking Spices

Regions: Napa, Sonoma, Bordeaux in France, Bolgheri in Italy

Cabernet Sauvignon is originally from France and is one of the most planted grape varieties in the world today. Its genesis starts as a cross between Cabernet Franc and Sauvignon Blanc. It is known for making full-body wines defined by big and robust tannins, usually wines that can age for several decades. These pair with grilled meats and rich, peppery sauces.

Suggested: Silver Oak Cabernet Sauvignon, Andis Cabernet Franc, or a Bordeaux Blend from the left bank

Other Grapes To Try: Merlot, Carmenere, Cabernet Franc, and Malbec

PINOT NOIR

Characteristics: Cherry, Rasberry, Mushroom, and Vanilla

Regions: Burgundy in France, Oregon, Marlborough in New Zealand

Pinot Noir is the most popular light-bodied red wine. Pinot Noir is a thin-skinned grape variety with moderate to high acidity, low to average levels of soft tannins, and is paler in color than most other red wines.

A red wine made from Pinot Noir has an aroma of red berries and cherry. Many of the more complex examples show hints of the forest floor.

An easy wine to pair with various types of cuisine, such as duck, chicken, and mushrooms.

Suggested: Nuits-St.-Georges 1er Cru "Clos des Porrets St. Georges," Henri Gouges, Sojourn Pinot Noir

Other Grapes To Try: Barbera d'Amador from Andis Wines, Grenache, Nerello Mascalase from Sicily, Gamay

SANGIOVESE & NEBBIOLO

Characteristics: Cherry, Rose, Leather, Espresso, and Oregano

Regions: Chianti, Montalcino, Montepulciano, Scansano for Sangiovese. Langhe, Barolo, Barbaresoc, Valtellina for Nebbiolo

Italy's most famous and acclaimed wines are made from these two grape varieties, Sangiovese and Nebbiolo. Sangiovese is the main grape grown in Tuscany and is responsible for making some of the best wines in the region. Chianti Classico, Brunello di Montalcino, and Nobile di Montepulciano are made using Sangiovese grape. Sangiovese wines are sensitive, balanced, and food friendly.

On the other hand, Barolo and Barbaresco are made from Nebbiolo grapes grown in Piedmont. These two regions deliver a Nebbiolo with delicate aromas and robust tannins age-worthy for up to 50 years.

Typical plates to pair with Sangiovese are tomato based dishes and well-spiced. Nebiolo tastes best with creamy cheese dishes and truffle notes.

Suggested: Brunello di Montalcino Uccelliera, Rosso Di Montepulciano, Barolo Domenico Clerico, Nebbiolo Langhe

Other Grapes To Try: Tempranillo, Aglianico, Xinomavro

ZINFANDEL, SYRAH, GSM BLEND & PETITE SIRAH

Characteristics: Blackberry, Strawberry, Sweet Tobacco, Plum, and Green Peppercorn

Regions: Lodi, Dry Creek, Sierra Foothills for Zinfandel. Passo Robles, North and South Rhone in France For Syrah and GSM, Napa Valley, Paso Robles, Amador County for Petite Sirah

Zinfandel is one of the oldest varieties grown in California. It makes fruit-forward yet bold wines with jammy fruit, smoky, exotic spices, and a hint of pepper. Originally from Croatia, it was made popular in Puglia as Primitivo and is now a California Classic. Zinfandel is ideal for BBQ, Mediterranean dishes, or a juicy burger.

Syrah and GSM blends are rich and powerful wines, sometimes meaty. GSM is a blend of Grenache, Syrah and Mourvedre. These grapes are typically grown in the Rhone region of France but are also very popular in the "new world," such as Australia and California. Darker meats and spices bring out the best notes of Syrah and GSM blends.

Petite Sirah is loved for its dark-colored wines with rich texture and robust tannins. Wines that are considered full body style. Petite Sirah is related to Syrah but makes a completely different style of wine. The best dishes to pair are fat and umami, steaks from the grill, and beef stroganoff.

Suggested: Painted Fields Old Vine Zinfandel Sierra Foothills, Tablas Creek Cotes Tables Red, Stags Leap Petite Sirah, Gigondas "Le Claux" Chateau Saint Cosme

Other Grapes To Try: Tannat, Sagrantino, Frappato, and Carignan

WHITES

White wine is my favorite category to drink. As a Winemaker and a winery owner, we value each other's jobs based on how good the white wines we produce are. It is an unappreciated category, considering how much attention we devote to producing delicious wines in a third of the time it takes to make red wine.

CHARDONNAY, VIOGNIER & RHONE GRAPES (GRENACHE BLANC, ROUSSANNE, MARSANNE)

Characteristics: Butter, Vanilla, Yellow Apple, Toast, Lemon Zest, Peach, Mango

Regions: Napa, Sonoma, and Santa Barbara in California, Burgundy in France, and Western Australia

Chardonnay is the world's most popular grape. This category of white wines is one of the most consumed in the market. These wines usually are aged in barrels to create a rich and oily, mostly buttery sensation on the palate. They are very complex wines to pair with food, considering their one-note flavor, BUTTER, They are great wines to have on their own, especially if you like semi-sweet wines.

Great food to pair with these wines is buttery and soft, like Lobster, Thai, or Vietnamese cuisine.

Suggested: Rombauer Chardonnay, Far Niente Chardonnay, Puligny-Montrachet, Bouchard Aîné

Other Grapes To Try: Andis Wines Semillon Bill Dillian Vineyard, Chablis, Rioja White Wine

SAUVIGNON BLANC, CHENIN BLANC, VERMENTINO & WHITE BORDEAUX BLEND

Characteristics: Gooseberry, Grapefruit, White Peach, Honey, Pear, Salt, Lemon

Regions: Loire Valley, Napa, New Zeland for Sauvignon Blanc. South Africa and Loire Valley for Chenin Blanc. Sadinia, Bolgheri for Vermentino Bordeaux for white bordeaux blends

This group of wines is known for their herbaceous flavors, low alcohol, perfume notes, and high acidity, making them the perfect sipper on hot summer days. Sauvignon Blanc is a white-wine grape from France, successfully grown in emerging and established wine regions worldwide. The variety produces lightly colored, dry white wines with fresh acidity.

Chenin Blanc, like Sauvignon Blanc, is originally from the western part of France, Loire Valley, and makes fantastic, dry summer whites and sparkling wines. It also offers oak-aged styles with flavors similar to Chardonnay.

Vermentino is a white wine grape grown in various

locations around the western Mediterranean. White wines often are light to medium-bodied, with flavor profiles similar to Sauvignon Blancs; they range from fresh and light-bodied white wines to rich textural ones depending on their style!

White Bordeaux blends are wines blended from Sauvignon Blanc, Semillon, and Muscadelle. Sauvignon brings grassy aromas to this blend, while Semillon adds a touch of complexity and a waxy, honeyed note. Muscadelle contributes grapey aromas.

Classic white Bordeaux blends are pale gold, with flashes of golden green, characterized by citrus, grass, and hay scents.

These wines pair well with grilled fish, mussels, and oysters.

Suggested: Antrinori Vermentino di Bolgheri, Sancerre "Les Terres Blanches", Domaine Gueneau, Ferrari-Carano Sauvignon Blanc, Vouvray Reserve du Naufraget Chenin Blanc

Other Grapes To Try: Albarino, Greco di Tufo, Picpoul, Vinho Verde

RIESLING & PINOT GRIGIO (PINOT GRIS)

Characteristics: Lime, Green Apple, Jasmine, Raw Almond, Lemon Zest

Regions: Mosel in Germany, Alsace in France, Washington, South Australia, and New York for Riesling. Friuli, Venice, Trentino Alto Adige in Italy, Oregon, Alsace in France, Australia

Riesling and Pinot Grigio are two of the world's oldest

grape varieties, and they are grown in very similar climates. Riesling and Pinot Grigio are medium-bodied white wines. Both wines are usually quite dry, but their fruitiness can trick the tongue into thinking they're a bit sweeter than reality.

Riesling is an aromatic white wine originally from Germany. White wines from Riesling vary in style, from off-dry to sweet wines. They pair very well with spices and Asian cuisine.

Pinot Gris, a.k.a Pinot Grigio, is a pink grape mutation from Pinot Noir, originally from France, but the North Italian style is very popular worldwide. Pinot Grigio makes an excellent pairing with white meats, seafood, or a great glass of wine as a happy hour.

Suggested: Kabinett "Ayler Kupp" Bischofliche Weinguter Trier, Peter Nicolay, Livio Felluga Pinot Grigio Colli Orientali del Friuli, Pinot Gris Ponzi Vineyards

Other Grapes To Try: Albarino, Friulano, Pinot Blanc, Muller Thurgau, Furmit

ROSÉS

Rosé is a type of wine that uses a fraction of a grape's skin color during production, making it different from red wines that use all the pigments. Rosé wines can are made from numerous different types of grapes. The rosé wine category has exploded in the last decade, from being a summer wine to now being an all-year-long presence in almost every restaurant menu worldwide.

LIGHT TO MEDIUM BODY ROSÉ

Characteristics: Grapefruit, Strawberry, Cherry, Rose

This category of Rosé wine is one of the most popular worldwide. They are usually made from thin skin varietals such as Pinot Noir, Gamay, Grenache, Mourvedre, or Cinsault. The color range from light pink salmon to just a few shades above it. They are best paired with light dishes, salads, or drunk as an aperitif.

Suggested; Rose from Provence or North Coast Pinot Noir Rose

MEDIUM BODY TO RICH

Characteristics: Raspberry, hibiscus, berry jam, and white pepper

Rosés from this category are made from thicker skin grapes, Syrah, Tempranillo, Zinfandel, or Cabernet Franc, and usually are darker shades of the rosé, in some cases closer to a light red wine. The texture of these wines is rich and could easily replace a red wine paired with dishes like grilled chicken, pork, or veggies.

Suggested: Rosé from Tavel in Rhone, Dry Zinfandel Rosé, or Syrah Rosé

SPARKLING WINE

Sparkling wines are a synonym for celebration. That long, classy glass called 'flute' filled with wine and tiny little bubbles puts a smile on our faces and energizes our moment. There are many ways to make them, and any grape varietal can be used from any region of the world. The wine can be white, rosé, or red, and the sweetness can range from dry to sweet. Considering that the Sparkling wine category is vast and has so many variations, we will group them into the most popular ones in the market.

CHAMPAGNE & TRADITIONAL METHOD A.K.A MÉTHODE CHAMPENOISE

Characteristics: Citrus, Yellow apple, Almond, Toast, Cream

The word 'champagne' is often used incorrectly when ordering wine. Most of the time, what we really mean is Sparkling Wine. Champagne is a sparkling wine made from the French region Champagne and is one of the most expensive sparkling wines in the market. The traditional method, a.k.a méthode champenoise, is made the same way as in Champagne but comes from other regions of the world. Most of the time is nonvintage, except for high-quality vintages, which can be white or rose, dry or off-dry, and rarely sweet.

Blanc de Blanc - white grapes only, Chardonnay mostly
Blanc de Noir - white from black grapes, Pinot Noir or Pinot Munier.

PROSECCO

Characteristics: Green Apple, Honeydew, Pera, Cream

It is Italy's most popular sparkling wine and is created by fermenting Glare grapes grown in Veneto and Friuli Venezia Giulia region. The best region known to produce prosecco is called Valdobbiadene. Like Champagne in France, Prosecco wine can only be made in Italy, and it varies in style from dry to sweet, and it can be white or rosé.

CAVA

Characteristics: Quine, Lime Yellow apple, Chamomile

Regions: Sparkling Wine is made almost made everywhere, but only a few regions succeed and make quality wines. Champagne, Loire, Alsace in France; Franciacorta, Valdobiadene, Asti in Italy; Catalonia in Spain

Cava is Spain's most quality sparkling wine and is made similarly to the Champagne method but using indigenous grapes grown in Spain. Also, Cava can be made as white wine or rose wine, and it has three major tiers that define the quality of the wine. Cava, Cava Reserva, and Cava Gran Reserve.

Lorenzo Muslia is the National Sales Manager and Partner of Andis Wines. The Andis winery is located in the rural wine region of Amador County California. You can join their wine club and find more information about the winery at: andiswines.com.

SHAKESPEARE'S CRAFT BEER & GASTRO PUB
3550 South Osprey Avenue
941-364-5938
shakespearesenglishpub.com

	BRITISH	**COST: $$**

HOURS: Daily, 11:30AM to 9PM

WHAT TO EXPECT: Great For After Work Meet-Up • Good For Lunch
Fantastic Burger • Traditional English Fare

BEST BITES: Black & Blue Burger • Tomato & Feta Salad
Caramelized Onion & Brie Burger • Cottage Pie
Bangers & Mash • English Fish & Chips

SCAN FOR MENU

SOME BASICS

Reservations:	NO
Spirits:	BEER/WINE
Parking:	LOT
Outdoor Dining:	YES

SHARKY'S ON THE PIER

1600 Harbor Drive South
941-488-1456
sharkysonthepier.com

VENICE	AMERICAN	COST: $$$

HOURS: Sun-Thur, 11:30AM to 10PM
Fri & Sat, 11:30AM to 11PM

WHAT TO EXPECT: Live Music • On The Beach • Very "Florida"
Voted Florida's Best Beach Bar ('13, '18, '19)

BEST BITES: NE Clam Chowder • Cabo Calamari • Sharky's Rice Bowl
Spiced Seafood Nachos • Boathouse Salad
Island Jambalaya • Captain Sharky's Platter

SOME BASICS

SCAN FOR MENU

Reservations:	YES
Spirits:	FULL BAR
Parking:	LOT
Outdoor Dining:	YES

SHORE

465 John Ringling Boulevard*
941-296-0301
dineshore.com

ST. ARMANDS	AMERICAN	COST: $$$

HOURS: Mon-Thur, 11AM to 10PM • Fri & Sat, 11AM to 11PM
Sun, 10AM to 10PM

WHAT TO EXPECT: Online Reservations • Busy During Season
Good Wine List • Happy Hour • Upscale Island Feel

BEST BITES: Tuna Tartare • Diner Meatloaf • Shore Burger
Vegan Kale 'Caesar' • Shrimp & Scallop
Grilled Branzino • Pasta Al Fresco • Thai Curry Mussels

SOME BASICS

SCAN FOR MENU

Reservations:	YES
Spirits:	FULL BAR
Parking:	STREET
Outdoor Dining:	YES

SIEGFRIED'S RESTAURANT

1869 Fruitville Road
941-330-9330
siegfrieds-restaurant.com

DOWNTOWN	GERMAN	COST: $$

HOURS: Wed-Sun, 4PM to 10PM
CLOSED MONDAY & TUESDAY

WHAT TO EXPECT: Casual Dining • Family Owned
Authentic German Cuisine • German Beer-Garden

BEST BITES: Wiener Schnitzel • Sauerbraten
Rheinische Reibekuchen • Leberkase Platter
Spatzle • German Schnitzel

SCAN FOR MENU

SOME BASICS

Reservations:	YES
Spirits:	BEER/WINE
Parking:	LOT/STREET
Outdoor Dining:	YES

SIESTA KEY OYSTER BAR (SKOB)

5238 Ocean Boulevard
941-346-5443
skob.com

SIESTA KEY	AMERICAN	COST: $$

HOURS: Mon-Thur, 11AM to 11PM • Fri & Sat, 11AM to 12AM
Sun, 9AM to 11PM

WHAT TO EXPECT: Vacation Atmosphere • Live Music Daily
Sunday Brunch • Great For Families • Busy In Season

BEST BITES: Tuna Poke Bites • Wings! • Crab Cakes
The SKOB Salad • Flatbreads • Big Boy Mac N Cheese
Chicken N' Waffles • Jill's Chicago Italian Beef

SCAN FOR MENU

SOME BASICS

Reservations:	NO
Spirits:	FULL BAR
Parking:	LOT/STREET
Outdoor Dining:	YES

SARASOTA SUSHI
YOUR BEST ROLLS ROLL HERE!

Looking for sushi in Sarasota? You're going to have a decision to make. We have some fantastic and creative sushi chefs that call Sarasota their home. We've got 20+ places where you can indulge. Space is limited here, so we have personally curated a list of some of the best places in town (subject to debate, of course). Whether, you're sitting at the bar or at a table with a group of friends, you can't go wrong with any of these places. Oh, just say "OMAKASE" and watch the magic happen...

DaRuMa Japanese Steak House • 5459 Fruitville Rd • 342-6600
WHAT TO EXPECT: Sushi + Teppan tableside cooking. This place is great for groups and big parties. Now open in The Landings.

Drunken Poet Cafe • 1572 Main St. • 955-8404
WHAT TO EXPECT: Sushi + Thai. A large selection of sushi. Downtown location. Also, lots of cooked options to choose from.

Jpan Restaurant • 3800 S. Tamiami Trl. • 954-5726
WHAT TO EXPECT: Always great. Never a miss here. BIG sushi menu. Super creative presentations. Also, across from UTC mall.

Kiyoshi's Sushi • 6550 Gateway Ave. • 924-3781
WHAT TO EXPECT: Nigiri, sashimi, and maki. That's pretty much it. This is a sushi restaurant. Very upscale creations & presentations.

Pacific Rim • 1859 Hillview St. • 330-0218
WHAT TO EXPECT: One of Sarasota's most established sushi restaurants. Good for groups. Lots of cooked dishes too.

Star Thai & Sushi • 240 Avenida Madera • 217-6758
WHAT TO EXPECT: Really creative & well presented sushi dishes. Lots of Thai choices as well. Friendly Siesta Key atmosphere.

Yume Sushi • 1537 Main St. • 363-0604
WHAT TO EXPECT: Downtown's go-to sushi place. Lots & lots of sushi. Also, a big assortment of other options. Great bar, too!

TUNA Tacoshimi

The Cottage is located in Siesta Key Village. Their menu focuses on inventive, seasonal cuisine from around the world.
More info at: cottagesiestakey.com

Illustration by Sarasota artist Bianca Colangelo.
Bianca is a Massachusetts native with a knack for being creative. Bianca spent her college years studying traditional processes designs and of ceramic arts and pottery.
More on her work at: Biancacolangeloceramics.bigcartel.com

SIMON'S COFFEE HOUSE

5900 South Tamiami Trail
941-926-7151
simonstogo.com

SOUTH TRAIL	DELI	COST: $$

HOURS: Mon-Sat, 8AM to 3PM
Sunday Brunch, 9AM to 3PM

WHAT TO EXPECT: Sandwiches • Salads • Homemade Soups
Lots Of Vegan & Vegetarian Options

BEST BITES: Fresh Juices • Crepes • Breakfast Toasted Sandwiches
Paninis • Vegetarian Burgers • Greek Salad
Spanakopita • Tex Mex Burger

SOME BASICS

SCAN FOR MENU

Reservations: NO
Spirits: BEER/WINE
Parking: LOT
Outdoor Dining: NO

SOUTHSIDE DELI

1825 Hillview Street
941-330-9302
southsidedelisarasota.com

SOUTHSIDE VILLAGE	DELI	COST: $$

HOURS: Mon-Fri, 7AM to 6PM • Sat, 7AM to 4PM
CLOSED SUNDAY

WHAT TO EXPECT: Deli Sandwiches • Quick Service
Great Salads • Drive Thru Service

BEST BITES: Burgers • Italian Chicken Sub • Fish & Chips
Paninis • Cuban Sandwich • Classic Reuben
Homemade Soup • Southsider Sandwich • Gyro

SOME BASICS

SCAN FOR MENU

Reservations: NO
Spirits: NONE
Parking: STREET
Outdoor Dining: YES

SPEAKS CLAM BAR

29 North Boulevard of Presidents*
941-232-7633
speaksclambar.com

ST. ARMANDS	SEAFOOD	COST: $$$

HOURS: Mon-Thur, 11AM to 10PM • Fri & Sat, 11AM to11PM
Sun, 12PM to 10PM

WHAT TO EXPECT: Clams! • "Italian" Clam Bar • Upscale But Casual
Gluten Free Menu • Good For Groups

BEST BITES: Raw Bar • Shrimp Arancini • Drunken Pei Mussels
Lobster Bisque • Maine Lobster Roll • Shrimp & Clam Bowl
Lasagna Bolognese • Chicken Marsala

SCAN FOR MENU

SOME BASICS
Reservations: YES
Spirits: FULL BAR
Parking: GARAGE/STREET
Outdoor Dining: YES

SPEARFISH GRILLE

1265 Old Stickney Point Road
941-349-1971
spearfishgrille.com

SIESTA KEY	SEAFOOD	COST: $$

HOURS: Daily, 11AM to 10PM

WHAT TO EXPECT: Super Casual • Island Feel
Fresh Seafood • Good For Families • Live Music

BEST BITES: Crispy Fried Grouper Cheeks • Tuna Poke
Fresh Gulf Hogfish • Cheesy Gulf Shrimp And Grits
Gulf Shrimp Po-Boy • Cuban Sammy

SCAN FOR MENU

SOME BASICS
Reservations: NONE
Spirits: FULL BAR
Parking: LOT/STREET
Outdoor Dining: YES

ST. ARMANDS OYSTER BAR

`NEW`

15 South Boulevard of the Presidents
941-388-1334
starmandsoysterbar.com

ST ARMANDS	SEAFOOD	COST: $$$

HOURS: Sun-Thur, 11AM to 9PM
Fri & Sat, 11AM to 12AM

WHAT TO EXPECT: Nola Cuisine • Super Relaxed But Upscale
Oyster Shucking Station • Busy Area During Season

BEST BITES: Blue Crab Cakes • Boiled Crawfish • Fresh Oysters!
Jambalaya • Crawfish Etoufee • Seafood Pasta
Po' Boy Sandwiches • Fried Catfish Platter

SOME BASICS

SCAN FOR MENU

Reservations:	NO
Spirits:	FULL BAR
Parking:	STREET/GARAGE
Outdoor Dining:	YES

SPICE STATION

1438 Boulevard of the Arts
941-343-2894
spicestationsrq.com

DOWNTOWN	THAI/SUSHI	COST: $$

HOURS: Lunch: Mon-Sat, 11AM to 3PM
Dinner: Mon-Sat 4:30PM to 9PM • CLOSED SUNDAY

WHAT TO EXPECT: Casual Asian Cuisine • Quaint And Comfortable
Vegetarian Options • Thai And Sushi • Nice Outdoor Space

BEST BITES: Thai Calamari • Panang Beef • Ginger Pork
Grouper With Ginger • Amazing Chicken
Tom Yum Goong • Duck With Chili & Basil • Sushi

SOME BASICS

SCAN FOR MENU

Reservations:	YES
Spirits:	BEER/WINE
Parking:	LOT/STREET
Outdoor Dining:	YES

STAR THAI AND SUSHI

240 Avenida Madera*
941-217-6758
starthaisushisiestakey.com

SIESTA KEY	ASIAN	COST: $$

HOURS: Wed-Mon, 12PM to 11PM
CLOSED TUESDAY

WHAT TO EXPECT: Sushi • Siesta Village • Very Friendly Staff
Live Music • Great For A Date

BEST BITES: Roasted Duck Noodle Soup • Sushi • Panang Curry
Crab Rangoon • Larb Gai • Tom Yum
Pad Thai • Soft Shell Crab • Three Buddies

SCAN FOR MENU

SOME BASICS

Reservations:	YES
Spirits:	FULL BAR
Parking:	STREET/LOT
Outdoor Dining:	YES

STATE STREET EATING HOUSE

1533 State Street
941-951-1533
statestreetsrq.com

DOWNTOWN	AMERICAN	COST: $$

HOURS: Tues-Fri, 5:30M to 11PM
Brunch: Sat & Sun, 10:30AM to 2:30PM

WHAT TO EXPECT: Great For A Date • Comfort Food • Good Wine List
Adult Lounge Scene • Excellent Cocktails

BEST BITES: Red Curry Mussels • Blistered Shishito Peppers
Pork Ragu • Prime Flat Iron Steak • Fried Chicken
State Street Burger • Hand Cut Garlic Parm Fries

SCAN FOR MENU

SOME BASICS

Reservations:	YES
Spirits:	FULL BAR
Parking:	STREET/GARAGE
Outdoor Dining:	YES

STATION 400

400 Lemon Avenue*
941-906-1400
station400.com

ROSEMARY DISTRICT	AMERICAN	COST: $$

HOURS: Daily, 7:30AM to 2:30PM

WHAT TO EXPECT: Great For Lunch Meet-Up • Lots Of Pancakes
Soups, Salads, & Sandwiches • Catering

BEST BITES: Bacon & Salted Caramel Pancakes • Nutella Waffle
Truffle Eggs Benedict • Greek Omelet • Reuben
Cobb Salad • Pressed French Dip • Falafel Wrap

SOME BASICS

SCAN FOR MENU

Reservations:	NO
Spirits:	BEER/WINE
Parking:	LOT
Outdoor Dining:	YES

STIKS

4413 South Tamiami Trail
941-923-2742
stiksfoods.com

SOUTH TRAIL	ASIAN	COST: $$

HOURS: Tue-Thur, 11:30AM to 8PM • Fri & Sun, 11:30AM to 8:30PM
CLOSED MONDAY

WHAT TO EXPECT: Fast Casual Asian Cuisine • Boba!
Lots Of Vegan Options • Great For A Quick Lunch

BEST BITES: Pad Thai • Shiitake Wide Noodles • Green Curry
Lao Curry Noodle Soup • Pho Beef Broth •
Fried Chicken Bites • Rangoons • Pork Dumplings

SOME BASICS

SCAN FOR MENU

Reservations:	NO
Spirits:	FULL BAR
Parking:	LOT
Outdoor Dining:	NO

STOTTLEMEYER'S SMOKEHOUSE

19 East Road
941-312-5969
stottlemyerssmokehouse.com

	BBQ	COST: $$

HOURS: Mon-Wed, 11:30AM to 8PM • Thur, 11:30AM to 9PM
Fri & Sat, 11:30PM to 10PM • Sun, 11:30AM to 9PM

WHAT TO EXPECT: Good For Families • Easy On The Wallet
Live Music • Casual Florida Dining Experience

BEST BITES: Fried Green Tomatoes • Smokehouse Salad
Beef Brisket • Famous Fried Chicken • Pulled Pork
Smoked Sausage Sandwich • Cuban Sandwich

SCAN FOR MENU

SOME BASICS
Reservations:	YES
Spirits:	FULL BAR
Parking:	LOT
Outdoor Dining:	YES

SUMMER HOUSE STEAK & SEAFOOD

149 Avenida Messina
941-260-2675
summerhousesiestakey.com

SIESTA KEY	STEAKHOUSE	COST: $$$

HOURS: Sun-Thur, 4PM to 10PM
Fri & Sat, 4PM to 11PM

WHAT TO EXPECT: Always Busy • Happy Hour • Upscale Dining
Fantastic Service • Excellent Wine List

BEST BITES: Colossal Shrimp Cocktail • Lobscargot
Lobster Bisque • Niman Ranch NY Strip • Filet Mignon
Diver Scallops • Pinot Noir Braised Short Rib

SCAN FOR MENU

SOME BASICS
Reservations:	YES
Spirits:	FULL BAR
Parking:	STREET/VALET
Outdoor Dining:	YES

SUN GARDEN CAFÉ
210 Avenida Madera
941-346-7170
sungardencafe.com

SIESTA KEY	AMERICAN	COST: $$

HOURS: Daily, 7:30AM to 1:30PM

WHAT TO EXPECT: Casual Island Lunch • Nice Outdoor Seating
Sandwich/Soup/Salad Combos

BEST BITES: Charleston Grits • Bikini Bagel • Garden Omelets
Shrimp Benedict • Adluh Mills Pancakes • Paninis
Curried Chicken Soup • Southern Fried Salad

SOME BASICS
SCAN FOR MENU

Reservations:	NO
Spirits:	BEER/WINE
Parking:	STREET
Outdoor Dining:	YES

TAHINI BEACH CAFE
NEW

103 Gulf Drive N.
941-251-4022
tahinibeachcafe.com

BRADENTON BEACH	MEDITERRANEAN	COST: $$

HOURS: Tues-Sun, 8:30AM to 3PM
CLOSED MONDAY

WHAT TO EXPECT: Breakfast & Lunch • Casual Beach Vibe
Great For A Carryout • Busy During Season

BEST BITES: Shakshuka • Tahini Beach Omelet • Tofu Scramble
Falafel Sandwich • Lamb Burger • Fattoush Salad
Baklava • Mango Custard • Rice Pudding

SOME BASICS
SCAN FOR MENU

Reservations:	NO
Spirits:	NONE
Parking:	STREET/LOT
Outdoor Dining:	YES

TAMIAMI TAP
711 South Osprey Avenue
941-500-3182
tamiamitap.com

LAUREL PARK	AMERICAN	COST: $$

HOURS: Tue-Sat, 4PM to 2AM • Sunday Brunch, 11AM to 3PM
CLOSED MONDAY

WHAT TO EXPECT: Casual & Fun! • Thursday Open Mic Night
Live Music • Nice Outdoor Dining Space

BEST BITES: Sliders • Hummus • Calamari Fries • Wings
Laurel Park Salad • Impossible Tacos • Shrimp Tacos
Steak Frites • Lobster Roll • Key Lime Pie

SCAN FOR MENU

SOME BASICS

Reservations:	NO
Spirits:	FULL BAR
Parking:	LOT
Outdoor Dining:	YES

TANDOOR
8453 Cooper Creek Boulevard
941-926-3077
tandoorsarasota.net

LWR	INDIAN	COST: $$

HOURS: Lunch: Tue-Sun, 11:30PM to 2:30PM
Dinner: Tue-Sun, 5PM to 9PM • CLOSED MONDAY

WHAT TO EXPECT: Upscale Atmosphere • Serving Since 2001
Authentic Traditional Indian Cuisine • Lots Of Parking

BEST BITES: Aloo Tikki • Paneer Pakora • Tikka Masala
Madras Curry • Chicken Makhani • Channa Masala
Aloo Saag • Chicken Biryani • Chicken Tandoori

SCAN FOR MENU

SOME BASICS

Reservations:	YES
Spirits:	FULL BAR
Parking:	LOT
Outdoor Dining:	NO

TOASTED MANGO CAFÉ

430 North Tamiami Trail*
941-388-7728
toastedmangocafe.com

NORTH TRAIL	AMERICAN	COST: $$

HOURS: Daily, 7:30AM to 2:30PM

WHAT TO EXPECT: Good For Families • Casual Dining • Great Service
Lots Of Menu Choices • Busy On Weekends

BEST BITES: Avocado Toast • Eggs Benedict • Biscuits And Gravy
Waffle N' Egg • Egg Salad Sandwich • Cobb Salad
The Debbie Sandwich • Smoked Salmon Platter

SOME BASICS

SCAN FOR MENU

Reservations: NO
Spirits: BEER/WINE
Parking: LOT
Outdoor Dining: NO

TOMMY BAHAMA RESTAURANT & BAR

300 John Ringling Boulevard
941-388-2888
tommybahama.com

ST. ARMANDS	AMERICAN	COST: $$

HOURS: Sun-Thur, 11AM to 8:30PM
Fri & Sat, 11AM to 9:30PM

WHAT TO EXPECT: Great For A Relaxing Lunch • Vacation Feel
Island Time Happy Hour • Online Reservations

BEST BITES: Macadamia-Crusted Goat Cheese • Brussels
All-American Burger • Thai Shrimp & Scallops
Jerk Chicken Tacos • World Famous Coconut Shrimp

SOME BASICS

SCAN FOR MENU

Reservations: YES
Spirits: FULL BAR
Parking: STREET
Outdoor Dining: YES

TONY'S CHICAGO BEEF

6569 Superior Avenue*
941-922-7979
tonyschicagobeef.com

GULF GATE	AMERICAN	COST: $

HOURS: Mon-Sat, 11AM to 9PM
CLOSED SUNDAY

WHAT TO EXPECT: Great For Lunch • Easy On The Wallet
Chicago Style Food • Counter And Table Seating

BEST BITES: Chicago Dog • Italian Beef Sandwich • Chicago Brat
Char-Grilled Burgers • Pork Chop Sandwich
Maxwell Street Polish Sausage • Pizza Puffs

SCAN FOR MENU

SOME BASICS

Reservations:	NO
Spirits:	BEER/WINE
Parking:	LOT/STREET
Outdoor Dining:	YES

EXPERIENCE A SARASOTA FOOD TOUR

KEY CULINARY TOURS

WHAT TO EXPECT: Culinary walking tours of neighborhoods in Sarasota, St. Armands, Anna Maria island and Venice. Lunch and dinner tours. A great opportunity to sample local foods; meet restaurateurs, discover Sarasota neighborhoods, and meet new friends! They're Sarasota's original culinary touring company.
MORE INFO: keyculinarytours.com or 941-893-4664

TASTE MAGAZINE PROGRESSIVE DINNERS

WHAT TO EXPECT: Remember the neighborhood progressive dinner? This your chance to experience an upgraded version of the classic food adventure. Taste Magazine sponsors themed progressive dinners about once every six weeks starting December 11th. Their walking historical and food tour of Bradenton departs every Wednesday & Thursday at 12PM. That's a fun way to spend a Florida afternoon.
MORE INFO: tasteweb.net or 941-366-7950

TRIPLETAIL SEAFOOD & SPIRITS

4870 South Tamiami Trail
941-529-0555
tripletailsrq.com

THE LANDINGS	SEAFOOD	COST: $$$

HOURS: Sun-Thur, 3PM to 9PM
Fri & Sat, 3PM to 10PM

WHAT TO EXPECT: Upscale, Casual Seafood • Happy Hour
Busy In Season • Handcrafted Cocktails

BEST BITES: Street Tacos • Lobster Mac & Cheese • Grouper Bites
Smoked Fish Dip • Fishcamp Chowder • Oysters
Tripletail • Crab Cakes • Ribeye Steak • Lobster Roll

SOME BASICS

SCAN FOR MENU

Reservations:	YES
Spirits:	FULL BAR
Parking:	LOT
Outdoor Dining:	YES

TURMERIC INDIAN BAR & GRILL   NEW

1001 Cocoanut Avenue
941-212-2622
turmericsarasota.com

ROSEMARY DIST	INDIAN	COST: $$$

HOURS: Mon, Wed, Thur, Sun, 11AM to 10PM
Fri & Sat, 11AM to 11PM • CLOSED TUESDAY

WHAT TO EXPECT: Indian "Fusion" Cuisine • Private Dining
Event Catering • Upscale Dining Atmosphere

BEST BITES: Dahi Aloo Puri • Lamb Boti Kebab • Momos
Chicken Tikka • Butter Chicken • Chana Masala
Dosa Stuffed • Biryani • Stuffed Naan

SOME BASICS

SCAN FOR MENU

Reservations:	YES
Spirits:	FULL BAR
Parking:	STREET
Outdoor Dining:	YES

TURTLES ON LITTLE SARASOTA BAY

8875 Midnight Pass Road
941-346-2207
turtlesrestaurant.com

SIESTA KEY	AMERICAN	COST: $$

HOURS: Mon-Sat, 11:30AM to 9PM
Sun, 10AM to 9PM

WHAT TO EXPECT: Right On The Water • Old Style Florida Dining
Sunday Brunch • Happy Hour Specials • Since 1986

BEST BITES: Coconut Shrimp • Turtles Wedge • NE Clam Chowder
Grouper Sandwich • Stuffed Shrimp • Fisherman Platter
Coconut Crusted Mahi Mahi • Turtle Pie

SCAN FOR MENU

SOME BASICS

Reservations:	YES
Spirits:	FULL BAR
Parking:	LOT
Outdoor Dining:	YES

VEG

6538 Gateway Avenue
941-312-6424
vegsrq.com

GULF GATE	VEGETARIAN	COST: $$

HOURS: Lunch, Mon-Sat, 11AM to 2PM
Dinner, Mon-Sat, 5PM to 8PM • CLOSED SUNDAY

WHAT TO EXPECT: Vegan/Veg • Daily Specials
One Of Sarasota's Oldest Vegetarian Restaurants

BEST BITES: Matzo Ball Soup • Vegan Mac N Cheese
Avocado Salad • Jackfruit Brisket Bowl • Silly Philly
Thai Peanut Tofu Wrap • Impossible Nacho Stack

SCAN FOR MENU

SOME BASICS

Reservations:	YES
Spirits:	BEER/WINE
Parking:	LOT/STREET
Outdoor Dining:	NO

VENEZIA

373 St Armands Circle
941-388-1400
venezia-1966.com

ST ARMANDS	ITALIAN	COST: $$

HOURS: Daily, 11PM to 10PM

WHAT TO EXPECT: Upscale Italian Bistro • Sidewalk Cafe Dining
No Reservations • Great For A Lunch Meetup

BEST BITES: Mussels Sautéed • Caprese Napoli • Calamari
Meatball Parmigiana • Gnocchi Alfredo
Grouper Francese • Pizza! • Salmon Ele

SOME BASICS

SCAN FOR MENU

Reservations:	NO
Spirits:	BEER/WINE
Parking:	STREET/GARAGE
Outdoor Dining:	YES

VERNONA

40 South Boulevard of the Presidents
941-254-5877
vernonagourmet.com

ST ARMANDS	HUNGARIAN	COST: $$$

HOURS: Mon-Sat, 11:30AM to 9PM
Sun, 7:30AM to 2:30PM

WHAT TO EXPECT: Gourmet Market • Pet Friendly
Upscale Casual Dining • Live Music

BEST BITES: BBQ Shrimp • Hungarian Crepes • Tomato Bisque
Chicken Panini • Beef Kabob • Stuffed Peppers
Avocado Toast • Quiche • French Toast

SOME BASICS

SCAN FOR MENU

Reservations:	YES
Spirits:	BEER/WINE
Parking:	LOT
Outdoor Dining:	NO

VERONICA FISH & OYSTER

1830 South Osprey Avenue
941-366-1342
veronicafishandoyster.com

SOUTHSIDE VILLAGE	SEAFOOD	COST: $$$

HOURS: Mon-Thur, 5PM to 9PM • Fri & Sat, 5PM to 10PM
CLOSED SUNDAY

WHAT TO EXPECT: Busy, Lively Dining Room • Handmade Cocktails
Raw Bar • Upscale Dining • Happy Hour

BEST BITES: Grilled Octopus • Bibb Salad • Smoked Fish Dip
Lobster Fra Diavolo • Pork Belly • Fresh Catch
Thai Crispy Whole Snapper • Blackened Mahi BLT

SCAN FOR MENU

SOME BASICS
Reservations:	YES
Spirits:	FULL BAR
Parking:	LOT/STREET
Outdoor Dining:	YES

ABOUT US

Way back in April 2002 we started dineSarasota as a way to bring up to date restaurant and dining information to Sarasota locals and visitors. Our annual printed dining guides and our website, dineSarasota.com, have grown right along with the ever expanding Sarasota dining scene. Whether you're just visiting or you're a native, we're here to help you make the most of your local dining experiences.

VILLAGE CAFÉ

5133 Ocean Boulevard
941-349-2822
villagecafeonsiesta.com

SIESTA KEY	AMERICAN	COST: $$

HOURS: Daily, 7:30AM to 2PM

WHAT TO EXPECT: Family Owned • Dog Friendly Outdoor Dining
Casual Dining • Open Since 1995 • Good For Families

BEST BITES: Belgian Waffles • Cinnamon Roll French Toast
The Works Omelet • Avocado Toast • Lox & Bagel
Burgers • Tom's Greek Salad • Daily Specials

SOME BASICS

SCAN FOR MENU

Reservations:	NO
Spirits:	BEER/WINE
Parking:	STREET
Outdoor Dining:	YES

WALT'S FISH MARKET AND RESTAURANT

4144 South Tamiami Trail
941-921-4605
waltsfishmarketrestaurant.com

SOUTH TRAIL	SEAFOOD	COST: $$

HOURS: Mon-Thur, 11AM to 9PM • Sun, 11AM to 10PM
Market, 9AM to 8PM

WHAT TO EXPECT: Restaurant & Market • Live Music • Casual Dining
Busy In Season • Since 1918!

BEST BITES: Stone Crab (in season) • Smoked Fish Spread
Peel & Eat Shrimp • Lobster Bisque • Oysters
Fresh Fish Daily • Off The Hook Oscar • Grouper Bowl

SOME BASICS

SCAN FOR MENU

Reservations:	NO
Spirits:	FULL BAR
Parking:	LOT
Outdoor Dining:	YES

LOCAL FARMERS MARKET INFORMATION

SARASOTA FARMERS MARKET
Lemon Avenue
Downtown Sarasota
Saturdays (Year Round)
7AM to 1PM
Rain or Shine
70+ Vendors
sarasotafarmersmarket.org

DOWNTOWN BRADENTON PUBLIC MARKET
Old Main Street (12 St. W)
Saturdays (October thru May)
9AM to 2PM
realizebradenton.com/about-the-market

SIESTA KEY FARMERS MARKET
Davidson's Plaza (5104 Ocean Boulevard)
Sundays (Year Round)
8AM to 12PM
Rain or Shine
siestakeyfarmersmarket.org

PHILLIPPI FARMHOUSE MARKET
Phillippi Estates Park (5500 South Tamiami Trail)
Wednesdays (October thru April)
9AM to 2PM
50+ Vendors
farmhousemarket.org

VENICE FARMERS MARKET
Venice City Hall (401 West Venice Avenue)
Saturdays (Year Round)
8AM to 12PM
thevenicefarmersmarket.org

WHAT'S IN SEASON?

Our Sarasota area farmer's markets really give locals and visitors a taste of fresh Florida flavor. But, our markets are more than a place just to stock up for the week. They're a place to mingle with friends, enjoy some music, or catch up on the latest neighborhood news!

Now you have a good list of places to buy the freshest locally grown produce. But, what's the best time of year to enjoy Florida's fruits and vegetables? When are they at their peak of freshness? Here's a little help.

WINTER > Bell Pepper • Eggplant • Grapefruit Strawberries • Squash • Tomatoes • Arugula • Kale
SPRING > Cantaloupe • Guava • Lettuce • Mushrooms Oranges • Papaya • Radish • Swiss Chard • Strawberries
SUMMER > Avocado • Guava • Mango • Eggplant Peanuts • Sweet Corn • Watermelon • Snow Peas
FALL > Cucumber • Grapefruit • Mushrooms • Lettuce Snap Beans • Tangerines • Tomatoes • Peppers

We have super fresh seafood here in Sarasota. You can usually find a plentiful supply of grouper, red snapper, pompano, and mahi at our farmer's markets. Of course, you can always find fresh Gulf shrimp in a variety of sizes.

The most anticipated seafood season runs from October 15th through May 1st. That's stone crab season! You're best off to grab these tasty delights towards the beginning of season when they're the most plentiful.

WICKED CANTINA

1603 North Tamiami Trail*
941-706-2395
wickedcantina.com

NORTH TRAIL	TEX MEX	COST: $$

HOURS: Daily, 11AM to 10PM

WHAT TO EXPECT: Casual Dining • Convenient Before A Show
Busy In Season • Happy Hour Daily

BEST BITES: Bar Taco Trio • Wicked Nachos • Cantina Dip
Cowboy Brisket Bowl • Chicken Tortilla Soup
Enchiladas • Tacos • Fajitas • Quesadillas

SCAN FOR MENU

SOME BASICS

Reservations:	YES
Spirits:	FULL BAR
Parking:	LOT
Outdoor Dining:	NO

WORD OF MOUTH

6604 Gateway Avenue
941-925-2400
originalwordofmouth.com

GULF GATE	AMERICAN	COST: $$

HOURS: Daily, 8AM to 2PM

WHAT TO EXPECT: Daily Specials • Casual Dining • Good For Families

BEST BITES: Fresh Baked Muffins • Smoothie Of The Day
Omelets • Frittatas • Eggs Benedict
Curried Egg Salad Sandwich • Classic BLT • Cobb Salad

SCAN FOR MENU

SOME BASICS

Reservations:	NO
Spirits:	BEER/WINE
Parking:	LOT/STREET
Outdoor Dining:	NO

YODER'S RESTAURANT
3434 Bahia Vista Street
941-955-7771
yodersrestaurant.com

PINECRAFT	AMISH	COST: $

HOURS: Mon-Sat, 7AM to 8PM
CLOSED SUNDAY

WHAT TO EXPECT: Great For Families • Easy On The Wallet
Busy In Season • Fantastic Service • Pie!!

BEST BITES: Daily Lunch, Dinner & Soup Specials • Great Sides!
Turkey Manhattan • Yoder's Famous Fried Chicken
Roast Turkey • Traditional BLT • Mom's Meatloaf

SOME BASICS
SCAN FOR MENU

Reservations:	NO
Spirits:	NONE
Parking:	LOT
Outdoor Dining:	NO

YOKOSO RAMEN
3422 Clark Road
941-265-1600
yokosoramen.com

NEW

	ASIAN	COST: $$

HOURS: Lunch & Dinner, Wed-Mon
CLOSED TUESDAY

WHAT TO EXPECT: REAL Ramen • Good For Families
Milk Teas • Lots Of Parking

BEST BITES: Gyoza • Shrimp Shumai • Yokoso Steamed Buns
Ramen Menu - Tonkotsu, Curry, Shoyu, Nabeyaki

SOME BASICS
SCAN FOR MENU

Reservations:	NO
Spirits:	NONE
Parking:	LOT
Outdoor Dining:	NO

YUME SUSHI

1532 Main Street
941-363-0604
yumerestaurant.com

DOWNTOWN	SUSHI	COST: $$

HOURS: Lunch, Mon-Sat, 11:30AM to 2PM
Dinner, Mon-Sun, 5PM to Close

WHAT TO EXPECT: Great For A Date • Fun Dining Experience
Great Sake Selection • Fantastic Service

BEST BITES: Daily Specials • Sushi • Sashimi • Hamachi Kama
Negimaki • Chicken Katsu • Tempura • Crispy Tartare
Tempura Udon Soup • Yume Tacos • Sake

SCAN FOR MENU

SOME BASICS

Reservations:	6 OR MORE
Spirits:	BEER/WINE
Parking:	STREET
Outdoor Dining:	NO

YUMMY HOUSE

1737 South Tamiami Trail
941-351-1688
yummyhouseflorida.com

SOUTH TRAIL	ASIAN	COST: $$

HOURS: Lunch, Daily, 11AM to 2:30PM
Dinner, Mon-Sat, 5PM to 9:30PM • Sun, 5PM to 9PM

WHAT TO EXPECT: Busy In Season • Lively Atmosphere
Lots Of Parking

BEST BITES: Salt & Pepper Shrimp • Peking Duck • Pot Stickers
Egg Drop Soup • Kung Po Chicken • Spicy XO Beef
Szechuan Style Pork • Clams With Black Bean Sauce

SCAN FOR MENU

SOME BASICS

Reservations:	YES
Spirits:	FULL BAR
Parking:	LOT
Outdoor Dining:	NO

Restaurant Name	Address	Phone #
A Sprig of Thyme	1962 Hillview St	330-8890
Almazonica Cerveceria	4141 S Tamiami Trl	260-5964
Alpine Steakhouse	4520 S Tamiami Trl	922-3797
Ama La Vlta Ristorante	1551 Main St	960-1551
Amore	180 N Lime Ave	383-1111
Andrea's	2085 Siesta Dr	951-9200
Anna Maria Oyster Bar	6696 Cortez Rd	792-0077
Anna Maria Oyster Bar	1525 51st Ave E	721-7773
Anna's Deli	6535 Midnight Pass	348-4888
Apollonia Grill	8235 Cooper Creek	359-4816
Athen's Family Rest.	2300 Bee Ridge Rd	706-4121
Atmosphere	935 N Beneva Rd	203-8542
Baby Brie's Cafe	1938 Adams Ln	362-0988
Baker & Wife	2157 Siesta Dr	960-1765
Bavaro's Pizza	27 Fletcher Ave	552-9131
Beach Bistro	6600 Gulf Dr N	778-6444
Beach House Restaurant	200 Gulf Dr N	779-2222
Bevardi's Salute!	23 N Lemon Ave	365-1020
Big Water Fish Market	6641 Midnight Pass	554-8101
Bijou Garden Café	1287 First St	366-8111
Blu Kouzina	25 N Blvd of Pres	388-2619
Blue Koi	3801 Macintosh Rd	388-7738
BLVD Cafe	1580 Blvd of the Arts	203-8102
Boca Sarasota	21 S Lemon Ave	256-3565
Bohemios Tapas Bar	3246 Clark Rd	260-9784
The Breakfast Company	7246 55th Ave E	201-6002
Bonjour French Cafe	5214 Ocean Blvd	346-0600
The Breakfast House	1817 Fruitville Rd	366-6860

Restaurant Name	Address	Phone #
BrewBurgers Pub	360 Commercial Ct	484-2337
Brick's Smoked Meats	1528 State St	993-1435
Brine Seafood	2250 Gulf Gate Dr	404-5639
Brooklyn Bagels & Deli	6970 S Beneva Rd	993-1577
Bushido Izayaki	3688 Webber St	217-5635
Buttermilk Handcrafted	5520 Palmer Blvd	487-8949
Café Barbosso	5501 Palmer Crossing	922-7999
Café Epicure	1298 Main St	366-5648
Café Gabbiano	5104 Ocean Blvd	349-1423
Café L'Europe	431 St Armands Cir	388-4415
Capt. Curt's Oyster Bar	1200 Old Stickney Pt	349-3885
Caragiulos	69 S Palm Ave	951-0866
Casey Key Fish House	801 Blackburn Pt Rd	966-1901
C'est La Vie!	1553 Main St	906-9575
Cha Cha Coconuts	417 St Armands Cir	388-3300
Chateau 13	535 13th St W	226-0110
Circo	1435 2nd St	253-0978
Clasico Italian Chophse	1341 Main St	957-0700
Clayton's Siesta Grille	1256 Old Stickney Pt	349-2800
The Columbia	411 St Armands Cir	388-3987
Connors Steakhouse	3501 S Tamiami Trl	260-3232
The Cottage	153 Avenida Messina	312-9300
Crab & Fin	420 St Armands Cir	388-3964
The Crow's Nest	1968 Tarpon Ctr Dr	484-9551
Curry Station	3550 Clark Rd	924-7222
Daiquiri Deck Raw Bar	5250 Ocean Blvd	349-8697
Daiquiri Deck Raw Bar	325 John Ringling Blvd	388-3325

Restaurant Name	Address	Phone #
Daiquiri Deck Raw Bar	300 W Venice Ave	488-0649
Daiquiri Deck Raw Bar	1250 Stickney Pt Rd	312-2422
DaRuMa Japanese	5459 Fruitville Rd	342-6600
DaRuMa Japanese	4910 S. Tamiami Trl	552-9465
Demetrio's Pizzeria	4410 S Tamiami Trl	922-1585
Der Dutchman	3713 Bahia Vista	955-8007
Dim Sum King	8194 Tourist Center Dr	306-5848
Doggystyle	1544 Main St	260-5835
Dolce Italia	6606 Superior Ave	921-7007
Drift Kitchen	700 Benjamin Franklin	388-2161
Drunken Poet Café	1572 Main St	955-8404
Dry Dock Waterfront	412 Gulf of Mexico Dr	383-0102
Dutch Valley Restaurant	6731 S Tamiami Trl	924-1770
Duval's, Fresh, Local...	1435 Main St	312-4001
El Melvin Cocina	1355 Main St	366-1618
El Toro Bravo	3218 Clark Rd	924-0006
Euphemia Haye	5540 Gulf of Mexico Dr	383-3633
1592 Wood Fired Kitch	1592 Main St	365-2234
481 Gourmet	481 N Orange Ave	362-0400
Faicco's Italian Hero's	3590 Webber St	960-1395
Figaro Bistro	1944 Hillview St	960-2109
Fins At Sharky's	1600 Harbor Dr S	999-3467
Flavio's Downtown	1766 Main St	960-2305
Flavio's Siesta Key	5239 Ocean Blvd	349-0995
Flirt Sushi Lounge	1296 First St	343-2122
Food + Beer	6528 Superior Ave	952-3361
Fork & Hen	2801 N Tamiami Trl	960-1212
Fresh Start Cafe	630 S Orange Ave	373-1242

Restaurant Name	Address	Phone #
Fushipoke	128 N Orange Ave	330-1795
Gecko's Grill & Pub	6606 S Tamiami Trl	248-2020
Gecko's Grill & Pub	5588 Palmer Crossing	923-6061
Gecko's Grill & Pub	351 N Cattlemen Rd	378-0077
Gecko's Grill & Pub	1900 Hillview St	953-2929
Gentile Cheesesteaks	7523 S Tamiami Trl	926-0441
Gilligan's Island Bar	5253 Ocean Blvd	349-4759
Good Liquid Brewing	1570 Lakefront Dr	238-6466
Grandpa's Schnitzel	2700 Stickney Pt Rd	922-3888
The Grasshopper	7253 S Tamiami Trl	923-3688
Graze Street AMI	3218 E Bay Dr	896-6320
GROVE Restaurant	10670 Boardwalk Lp	893-4321
Harry's Continental Kit.	525 St Judes Dr	383-0777
Hob Nob Drive-In	1701 Washington Blvd	955-5001
The Hub Baha Grill	5148 Ocean Blvd	349-6800
Il Panificio	1703 Main St	366-5570
Il Panificio	215 Avenida Madera	800-5570
Indigenous	239 Links Ave	706-4740
Inkawasi Peruvian	10667 Boardwalk Lp	360-1110
Island House Tap & Grl.	5110 Ocean Blvd	312-9205
Island House Taqueria	2773 Bee Ridge Rd	922-8226
Jack Dusty	1111 Ritz-Carlton Dr	309-2266
Jersey Girl Bagels	5275 University Pkwy	388-8910
Joey D's Chicago Style	3811 Kenny Dr.	378-8900
Jpan Sushi & Grill	3 Paradise Plaza	954-5726
Jpan Sushi & Grill	229 N Cattlemen Rd	954-5726
JR's Old Packinghouse	987 S Packinghse Rd	371-9358

Restaurant Name	Address	Phone #
Ka Papa Cuisine	1830 S Osprey Ave	600-8590
Kacey's Seafood	4904 Fruitville Rd	378-3644
Kiyoski's Sushi	6550 Gateway Ave	924-3781
Knick's Tavern & Grill	1818 S Osprey Ave	955-7761
Kojo	1289 N Palm Ave	536-9717
Kore Steakhouse	1561 Lakefront Dr	928-5673
Lazy Lobster	5350 Gulf of Mexico Dr	388-0440
Libby's Bistro	1917 S Osprey Ave	487-7300
Lila	1576 Main St	296-1042
Little Saigon Bistro	2725 S Beneva Rd	312-4730
The Lobster Pot	5157 Ocean Blvd	349-2323
Lobstercraft	28 S Blvd of Pres	346-6325
Lovely Square	6559 Gateway Ave	724-2512
Made	1990 Main St	953-2900
Mademoiselle Paris	8527 Cooper Creek Bl	355-2323
Mademoiselle Paris	1605 Main St	544-4021
Madfish Grill	4059 Cattlemen Rd	377-3474
Madison Avenue Deli	28 N Blvd of Pres	388-3354
Main Bar Sandwich Shop	1944 Main St	955-8733
Maison Blanche	2605 Gulf of Mexico Dr	383-8088
Mar-Vista Restaurant	760 Broadway St	383-2391
Marcello's Ristorante	4155 S Tamiami Trl	921-6794
Marina Jack's	2 Marina Plaza	365-4243
Mattison's City Grille	1 N Lemon Ave	330-0440
Mattison's Forty One	7275 S Tamiami Trl	921-3400
Mediterraneo	1970 Main St	365-4122

Restaurant Name	Address	Phone #
Melange	1568 Main St	953-7111
Meliora	1920 Hillview St	444-7692
Michael John's	1040 Carlton Arms	747-8032
Michael's On East	1212 East Ave	366-0007
Michelle's Brown Bag	1819 Main St	365-5858
Miguel's	6631 Midnight Pass	349-4024
Molly's Pub	1562 Main St	366-7711
Millie's Cafe	3900 Clark Rd	923-4054
Monk's Steamer Bar	6690 Superior Ave	927-3388
Munchies 420 Café	6639 Superior Ave	929-9893
99 Bottles Taproom	1445 2nd St	487-7874
Nancy's Bar-B-Que	14475 SR 70	999-2390
Napule Ristorante	7129 S Tamiami Trl	556-9639
Nellie's Deli & Market	15 S Beneva Rd	924-2705
New Pass Grill	1505 Ken Thompson	388-3050
Nicky's On Palm	49 S Palm Ave	330-1727
Oak & Stone	5405 University Pkwy	225-4590
Oak & Stone	4067 Clark Rd	893-4881
Oasis Café	3542 S Osprey Ave	957-1214
The Old Salty Dog	5023 Ocean Blvd	349-0158
The Old Salty Dog	160 Ken Thompson Pk	388-4311
The Old Salty Dog	1485 S Tamiami Trl	483-1000
O'Leary's Tiki Bar	5 Bayfront Dr	953-7505
Ophelia's on the Bay	9105 Midnight Pass	349-2212
Opus Restaurant	6644 Gateway Ave	925-2313
Origin Beer & Pizza	3837 Hillview St	316-9222
Origin Beer & Pizza	5070 Clark Rd	217-6533

Restaurant Name	Address	Phone #
Origin Beer & Pizza	8193 Tourist Ctr Dr	358-5850
Ortygia	1418 13th St W	741-8646
Owen's Fish Camp	516 Burns Ct	951-6936
Pacific Rim	1859 Hillview St	330-8071
Parrot Patio Bar & Grill	3602 Webber St	952-3352
Pastry Art Bakery	1512 Main St	955-7545
Patrick's 1481	1481 Main St	955-1481
Phillippi Creek Oyster	5363 S Tamiami Trl	925-4444
Pho Cali	1578 Main St	955-2683
Piccolo Italian Market	6518 Gateway Ave	923-2202
Pier 22	1200 1st Avenue W	748-8087
Pizza N' Brew	1507 Main St	359-3894
Pizza N' Brew	6645 Midnight Pass	349-4490
The Point	135 Bayview Dr	218-6114
Pop's Sunset Grill	112 Circuit Rd	488-3177
Prime Serious Steak	133 S Tamiami Trl	837-8325
The Public House	6240 N Lockwood Rg	822-0795
Reef Cakes	1812 S Osprey Ave	444-7968
Reyna's Taqueria	935 N Beneva Rd	260-8343
Rick's French Bistro	2177 Siesta Dr	957-0533
Ripfire Pizza & BBQ	5218 Ocean Blvd	313-7511
Riverhouse Reef & Grill	995 Riverside Dr	729-0616
Rodizio Grill	5911 Fruitville Rd	260-8445
Roessler's	2033 Vamo Way	966-5688
RomanSQ	6670 Superior Ave	237-8742
Rosebud's Steakhouse	2215 S Tamiami Trl	918-8771
The Rosemary	411 N Orange Ave	955-7600
Rosemary & Thyme	511 N Orange Ave	955-7600

Restaurant Name	Address	Phone #
Sage	1216 1st St	445-5660
Sardinia	5770 S Tamiami Trl	702-8582
Schnitzel Kitchen	6521 Superior Ave	922-9299
Screaming Goat Taq.	6606 Superior Ave	210-3992
Selva Grill	1345 Main St	362-4427
Shakespeare's Eng. Pub	3550 S Osprey Ave	364-5938
Shaner's Pizza	6500 Superior Ave	927-2708
Sharky's on the Pier	1600 Harbor Dr S	488-1456
Shore Diner	465 John Ringling	296-0303
Siegfried's Restaurant	1869 Fruitville Rd	330-9330
Siesta Key Oyster Bar	5238 Ocean Blvd	346-5443
Simon's Coffee House	5900 S Tamiami Trl	926-7151
Southside Deli	1825 Hillview St	330-9302
Speaks Clam Bar	29 N Blvd of Pres.	232-7633
Spearfish Grille	1265 Old Stickney Pt	349-1970
Spice Station	1438 Blvd of the Arts	343-2894
St. Armands Oyster Bar	15 S Blvd of Pres	388-1334
Star Thai & Sushi	240 Avenida Madera	217-6758
State St. Eating House	1533 State St	951-1533
Station 400	400 Lemon Ave	906-1400
Station 400	8215 Lakewood Main	907-0648
Stiks	4413 S Tamiami Trl	923-2742
Stottlemeyer's Smokehs	19 East Rd	312-5969
The Summer House	149 Avenida Messina	206-2675
Sun Garden Café	210 Avenida Madera	346-7170
Tahini Beach Cafe	103 Gulf Dr N	251-4022
Tamiami Tap	711 S Osprey Ave	500-3182
Tandoor	8453 Cooper Creek	926-3070

Restaurant Name	Address	Phone #
Toasted Mango Café	430 N Tamiami Trl	388-7728
Toasted Mango Café	6621 Midnight Pass	552-6485
Tommy Bahama Café	300 John Ringling Blvd	388-2888
Tony's Chicago Beef	6569 Superior Ave	922-7979
Tony's Chicago Beef	1856 S Tamiami - Ven.	497-1611
Tripletail Seafood	4870 S Tamiami Trl	529-0555
Turmeric	1001 Cocoanut Ave	212-2622
Turtle's	8875 Midnight Pass	346-2207
Veg	2164 Gulf Gate Dr	312-6424
Venizia	373 St Armands Cir	388-1400
Vernona	40 S Blvd of Pres	254-5877
Veronica Fish & Oyster	1830 S Osprey Ave	366-1342
Village Café	5133 Ocean Blvd	349-2822
Walt's Fish Market	4144 S Tamiami Trl	921-4605
Wicked Cantina	1603 N Tamiami Trl	821-2990
Word of Mouth	6604 Gateway Ave	925-2400
Yoder's Restaurant	3434 Bahia Vista	955-7771
Yokoso Ramen	3422 Clark Rd	265-1600
Yume Sushi	1532 Main St	363-0604
Yummy House	1737 S Tamiami Trl	351-1688

Scan for the latest
Sarasota Restaurant
news. Subscribe to
our newsletter

**sarasota
bites**

AMERICAN		
Restaurant Name	Address	Phone #
Baby Brie's Cafe	1938 Adams Ln	362-0988
Baker & Wife	2157 Siesta Dr	960-1765
Beach Bistro	6600 Gulf Dr N	778-6444
Beach House Rest.	200 Gulf Dr N	779-2222
Bijou Café	1287 First St	366-8111
BLVD Cafe	1580 Blvd of the Arts	203-8102
Boca Sarasota	21 S. Lemon Ave	256-3565
The Breakfast Company	7246 55th Ave E	201-6002
The Breakfast House	1817 Fruitville Rd	366-6860
Brick's Smoked Meats	1528 State St	993-1435
BrewBurgers Pub	360 Commercial Ct	484-2337
Buttermilk Handcrafted	5520 Palmer Blvd	487-8949
Cha Cha Coconuts	417 St Armands Cir	388-3300
Clayton's Siesta Grille	1256 Old Stickney Pt	349-2800
The Cottage	153 Avenida Messina	312-9300
Daiquiri Deck Raw Bar	5250 Ocean Blvd	349-8697
Daiquiri Deck Raw Bar	325 John Ringling Blvd	388-3325
Daiquiri Deck Raw Bar	300 W Venice Ave	488-0649
Daiquiri Deck Raw Bar	1250 Stickney Pt Rd	312-2422
Doggystyle	1544 Main St	260-5835
Drift Kitchen	700 Benjamin Franklin	388-2161
Der Dutchman	3713 Bahia Vista	955-8007
Dutch Valley Restaurant	6731 S Tamiami Trl	924-1770
Duval's, Fresh, Local...	1435 Main St	312-4001
Euphemia Haye	5540 Gulf of Mexico Dr	383-3633
481 Gourmet	481 N Orange Ave	362-0400

AMERICAN		
Restaurant Name	**Address**	**Phone #**
Food + Beer	6528 Superior Ave	952-3361
Fork & Hen	2801 N Tamiami Trl	960-1212
Gecko's Grill & Pub	6606 S Tamiami Trl	248-2020
Gecko's Grill & Pub	1900 Hillview St	953-2929
Gecko's Grill & Pub	5588 Palmer Crossing	923-6061
Gecko's Grill & Pub	351 N Cattlemen Rd	378-0077
Gentile Cheesesteaks	7523 S Tamiami Trl	926-0441
Gilligan's Island Bar	5253 Ocean Blvd	349-4759
Good Liquid Brewing	1570 Lakefront Dr	238-6466
Graze Street AMI	3218 E Bay Dr	896-6320
GROVE Restaurant	10670 Boardwalk Lp	893-4321
Harry's Continental Kit.	525 St Judes Dr	383-0777
Hob Nob Drive-In	1701 Washington Blvd	955-5001
The Hub Baha Grill	5148 Ocean Blvd	349-6800
Indigenous	239 Links Ave	706-4740
Island House Tap & Grl.	5110 Ocean Blvd	312-9205
Jack Dusty	1111 Ritz-Carlton Dr	309-2266
Joey D's Chicago Style	3811 Kenny Dr.	378-8900
JR's Old Packinghouse	987 S Packinghouse	371-9358
Knick's Tavern & Grill	1818 S Osprey Ave	955-7761
Libby's	1917 S Osprey Ave	487-7300
Lovely Square	6559 Gateway Ave	724-2512
Made	1990 Main St	953-2900
Madfish Grill	4059 Cattlemen Rd	377-3474
Marina Jack's	2 Marina Plaza	365-4243
Mattison's City Grille	1 N Lemon Ave	330-0440

AMERICAN		
Restaurant Name	**Address**	**Phone #**
Mattison's Forty One	7275 S Tamiami Trl	921-3400
Meliora	1920 Hillview St	444-7692
Melange	1568 Main St	953-7111
Michael John's	1040 Carlton Arms	747-8032
Michael's On East	1212 East Ave	366-0007
Millie's Cafe	3900 Clark Rd	923-4054
Munchies 420 Café	6639 Superior Ave	929-9893
99 Bottles Taproom	1445 2nd St	487-7874
Nancy's Bar-B-Que	14475 SR 70	999-2390
New Pass Grill	1505 Ken Thompson	388-3050
Nicky's On Palm	49 S Palm Ave	330-1727
Oak & Stone	5405 University Pkwy	225-4590
Oak & Stone	4067 Clark Rd	893-4881
Oasis Cafe	3542 S Osprey Ave	957-1214
The Old Salty Dog	5023 Ocean Blvd	349-0158
The Old Salty Dog	160 Ken Thompson Pk	388-4311
The Old Salty Dog	1485 S Tamiami Trl	483-1000
O'Leary's Tiki Bar	5 Bayfront Dr	953-7505
Ophelia's on the Bay	9105 Midnight Pass	349-2212
Opus Restaurant	6644 Gateway Ave	925-2313
Parrot Patio Bar & Grill	3602 Webber St	952-3352
Pastry Art Bakery	1512 Main St	955-7545
Patrick's 1481	1481 Main St	955-1481
Pier 22	1200 1st Avenue W	748-8087
Pizza N' Brew	1507 Main St	359-3894
Pizza N' Brew	6645 Midnight Pass	349-4490

AMERICAN		
Restaurant Name	**Address**	**Phone #**
The Point	135 Bayview Dr	218-6114
Pop's Sunset Grill	112 Circuit Rd	488-3177
The Public House	6240 N Lockwood Rg	822-0795
The Rosemary	411 N Orange Ave	955-7600
Rosemary & Thyme	511 N Orange Ave	955-7600
Sage	1216 1st St	445-5660
The Sandbar	100 Spring Ave	778-0444
Sharky's on the Pier	1600 Harbor Dr S	488-1456
Shore Diner	465 John Ringling Blvd	296-0303
Siesta Key Oyster Bar	5238 Ocean Blvd	346-5443
State St. Eating House	1533 State St	951-1533
Station 400	400 Lemon Ave	906-1400
Station 400	8215 Lakewood Main	907-0648
Stottlemeyer's Smokehs	19 East Rd	312-5969
Sun Garden Cafe	210 Avenida Madera	346-7170
Tahini Beach Cafe	103 Gulf Dr N	251-4022
Tamiami Tap	711 S Osprey Ave	500-3182
Toasted Mango Café	6621 Midnight Pass	552-6485
Toasted Mango Café	430 N Tamiami Trl	388-7728
Tommy Bahama Café	300 John Ringling Blvd	388-2888
Tony's Chicago Beef	6569 Superior Ave	922-7979
Turtle's	8875 Midnight Pass	346-2207
Village Café	5133 Ocean Blvd	349-2822
Word of Mouth	6604 Gateway Ave	925-2400
Yoder's Restaurant	3434 Bahia Vista	955-7771

ASIAN		
Restaurant Name	Address	Phone #
Blue Koi	3801 Macintosh Rd	388-7738
DaRuMa Japanese	4910 S. Tamiami Trl	552-9465
Dim Sum King	8194 Tourist Center Dr	306-5848
Drunken Poet Café	1572 Main St	955-8404
Flirt Sushi Lounge	1296 First St	343-2122
Fushipoke	128 N Orange Ave	330-1795
Jpan Sushi & Grill	3 Paradise Plaza	954-5726
Jpan Sushi & Grill	229 N Cattlemen Rd	954-5726
Kiyoski's Sushi	6550 Gateway Ave	924-3781
Kojo	1289 N Palm Ave	536-9717
Kore Steakhouse	1561 Lakefront Dr	928-5673
Little Saigon Bistro	2725 S Beneva Rd	312-4730
Pacific Rim	1859 Hillview St	330-8071
Pho Cali	1578 Main St	955-2683
Spice Station	1438 Blvd of the Arts	343-2894
Star Thai & Sushi	240 Avenida Madera	217-6758
Stiks	4413 S Tamiami Trl	923-2742
Yokoso Ramen	3422 Clark Rd	265-1600
Yume Sushi	1532 Main St	363-0604
Yummy House	1737 S Tamiami Trl	351-1688

CUBAN, MEXICAN & SPANISH		
Bohemios Tapas Bar	3246 Clark Rd	260-9784
Circo	1435 2nd St	253-0978
The Columbia	411 St Armands Cir	388-3987
El Melvin Cocina	1355 Main St	366-1618
El Toro Bravo	2720 Stickney Pt Rd	924-0006

CUBAN, MEXICAN & SPANISH

Restaurant Name	Address	Phone #
The Grasshopper	7253 S Tamiami Trl	923-3688
Island House Taqueria	2773 Bee Ridge Rd	922-8226
Reyna's Taqueria	935 N Beneva Rd	260-8343
Screaming Goat Taq.	6606 Superior Ave	210-3992
Wicked Cantina	1603 N Tamiami Trl	821-2990

DELI

Anna's Deli	6535 Midnight Pass	348-4888
Brooklyn Bagels & Deli	6970 S Beneva Rd	993-1577
Faicco's Italian Hero's	3590 Webber St	960-1395
Gentile Cheesesteaks	7523 S Tamiami Trl	926-0441
Jersey Girl Bagels	5275 University Pkwy	388-8910
Madison Avenue Deli	28 N Blvd of Pres	388-3354
Main Bar Sandwich Shp	1944 Main St	955-8733
Michelle's Brown Bag	1819 Main St	365-5858
Nellie's Deli	15 S Beneva Rd	924-2705
Piccolo Italian Market	6518 Gateway Ave	923-2202
Simon's Coffee House	5900 S Tamiami Trl	926-7151
Southside Deli	1825 Hillview St	330-9302

ENGLISH, IRISH & SCOTTISH

Molly's Pub	1562 Main St	366-7711
Shakespeare's	3550 S Osprey Ave	364-5938

FRENCH

A Sprig of Thyme	1962 Hillview St	330-8890
Bonjour French Cafe	5214 Ocean Blvd	346-0600

FRENCH		
Restaurant Name	**Address**	**Phone #**
Chateau 13	535 13th St W	226-0110
Rick's French Bistro	2177 Siesta Dr	957-0533
C'est La Vie!	1553 Main St	906-9575
Figaro Bistro	1944 Hillview St	960-2109
Mademoiselle Paris	8527 Cooper Creek Bl	355-2323
Maison Blanche	2605 Gulf of Mexico Dr	383-8088
Miguel's	6631 Midnight Pass	349-4024
GREEK		
Apollonia Grill	8235 Cooper Creek	359-4816
Athen's Family Rest.	2300 Bee Ridge Rd	706-4121
Blu Kouzina	25 N Blvd of Pres	388-2619
1592 Wood Fired Kitch	1592 Main St	365-2234
INDIAN		
Curry Station	3550 Clark Rd	924-7222
Tandoor	8453 Cooper Creek	926-3070
Turmeric	1001 Cocoanut Ave	212-2622
ITALIAN		
Amore	180 N Lime Ave	383-1111
Andrea's	2085 Siesta Dr	951-9200
Atmosphere	935 N Beneva Rd	203-8542
Bevardi's Salute!	23 N Lemon Ave	365-1020
Café Barbosso	5501 Palmer Crossing	922-7999
Café Epicure	1298 Main St	366-5648

ITALIAN

Restaurant Name	Address	Phone #
Café Gabbiano	5104 Ocean Blvd	349-1423
Café L'Europe	431 St Armands Cir	388-4415
Caragiulos	69 S Palm Ave	951-0866
Clasico Italian Chophse	1341 Main St	957-0700
Dolce Italia	6606 Superior Ave	921-7007
Flavio's Brick Oven	5239 Ocean Blvd	349-0995
Marcello's Ristorante	4155 S Tamiami Trl	921-6794
Mediterraneo	1970 Main St	365-4122
Napule Ristorante	7129 S Tamiami Trl	556-9639
Piccolo Italian Market	6518 Gateway Ave	923-2202
Sardinia	5770 S Tamiami Trl	702-8582
Venizia	373 St Armands Cir	388-1400

SEAFOOD

Anna Maria Oyster Bar	6906 14th St W	758-7880
Anna Maria Oyster Bar	6696 Cortez Rd	792-0077
Big Water Fish Market	6641 Midgnight Pass	554-8101
Brine Seafood	2250 Gulf Gate Dr	404-5639
Capt. Curt's Oyster Bar	1200 Old Stickney Pt	349-3885
Casey Key Fish House	801 Blackburn Pt Rd	966-1901
Crab & Fin	420 St Armands Cir	388-3964
The Crow's Nest	1968 Tarpon Ctr Dr	484-9551
Dry Dock Waterfront	412 Gulf of Mexico Dr	383-0102
Duval's, Fresh, Local...	1435 Main St	312-4001
Fins At Sharky's	1600 Harbor Dr S	999-3467
Kacey's Seafood	4904 Fruitville Rd	378-3644

SEAFOOD		
Restaurant Name	**Address**	**Phone #**
Lazy Lobster	5350 Gulf of Mexico Dr	388-0440
Lobstercraft	28 S Blvd of Pres	346-6325
The Lobster Pot	5157 Ocean Blvd	349-2323
Mar-Vista Restaurant	760 Broadway St	383-2391
Monk's Steamer Bar	6690 Superior Ave	927-3388
Ophelia's on the Bay	9105 Midnight Pass	349-2212
Owen's Fish Camp	516 Burns Ct	951-6936
Phillippi Creek Oyster	5363 S Tamiami Trl	925-4444
Reef Cakes	1812 S Osprey Ave	444-7968
St. Armands Oyster Bar	15 S Blvd of Pres	388-1334
Siesta Key Oyster Bar	5238 Ocean Blvd	346-5443
Speaks Clam Bar	29 N Blvd of Pres.	232-7633
Spearfish Grille	1265 Old Stickney Pt	349-1970
Tripletail Seafood	4870 S Tamiami Trl	529-0555
Veronica Fish & Oyster	1830 S Osprey Ave	366-1342
Walt's Fish Market	4144 S Tamiami Trl	921-4605
STEAKHOUSE		
Alpine Steakhouse	4520 S Tamiami Trl	922-3797
Connors Steakhouse	3501 S Tamiami Trl	260-3232
Rosebud's Steakhouse	2215 S Tamiami Trl	918-8771
The Summer House	149 Avenida Messina	206-2675

ANNA MARIA, BRADENTON, & PALMETTO		
Restaurant Name	Address	Phone #
Beach Bistro	6600 Gulf Dr N	778-6444
The Breakfast Company	7246 55th Ave E	201-6002
Chateau 13	535 13th St W	226-0110
Graze Street AMI	3218 E Bay Dr	896-6320
Tahini Beach Cafe	103 Gulf Dr N	251-4022
Michael John's	1040 Carlton Arms	747-8032
Pier 22	1200 1st Avenue W	748-8087
DOWNTOWN		
Amore	180 N Lime Ave	383-1111
Baby Brie's Cafe	1938 Adams Ln	362-0988
Bavaro's Pizza	27 Fletcher Ave	552-9131
Bevardi's Salute!	23 N Lemon Ave	365-1020
Bijou Cafe	1287 First St	366-8111
BLVD Cafe	1580 Blvd of the Arts	203-8102
Boca Sarasota	21 S Lemon Ave	256-3565
The Breakfast House	1817 Fruitville Rd	366-6860
Brick's Smoked Meats	1528 State St	993-1435
Café Epicure	1298 Main St	366-5648
Caragiulos	69 S Palm Ave	951-0866
C'est La Vie!	1553 Main St	906-9575
Circo	1435 2nd St	253-0978
Clasico Italian Chophse	1341 Main St	957-0700
Doggystyle	1544 Main St	260-5835
Drunken Poet Café	1572 Main St	955-8404
Duval's, Fresh, Local...	1435 Main St	312-4001

DOWNTOWN		
Restaurant Name	Address	Phone #
El Melvin Cocina	1355 Main St	366-1618
1592 Wood Fired Kitch	1592 Main St	365-2234
481 Gourmet	481 N Orange Ave	362-0400
Flirt Sushi Lounge	1296 First St	343-2122
Fushipoke	128 N Orange Ave	330-1795
Il Panificio	1703 Main St	366-5570
Indigenous	239 Links Ave	706-4740
Jack Dusty	1111 Ritz-Carlton Dr	309-2266
Kojo	1289 N Palm Ave	536-9717
Lila	1576 Main St	296-1042
Made	1990 Main St	953-2900
Main Bar Sandwich Shp	1944 Main St	955-8733
Mandeville Beer Garden	428 N Lemon Ave	954-8688
Marina Jack's	2 Marina Plaza	365-4243
Mattison's City Grille	1 N Lemon Ave	330-0440
Mediterraneo	1970 Main St	365-4122
Melange	1568 Main St	953-7111
Michelle's Brown Bag	1819 Main St	365-5858
Molly's Pub	1562 Main St	366-7711
99 Bottles Taproom	1445 2nd St	487-7874
Nicky's On Palm	49 S Palm Ave	330-1727
O'Leary's Tiki Bar	5 Bayfront Dr	953-7505
Owen's Fish Camp	516 Burns Ct	951-6936
Pastry Art Bakery	1512 Main St	955-7545
Patrick's 1481	1481 Main St	955-1481
Pho Cali	1578 Main St	955-2683

DOWNTOWN

Restaurant Name	Address	Phone #
Pizza N' Brew	1507 Main St	359-3894
The Rosemary	411 N Orange Ave	955-7600
Rosemary & Thyme	511 N Orange Ave	955-7600
Sage	1216 1st St	445-5660
Selva Grill	1345 Main St	362-4427
Siegfried's Restaurant	1869 Fruitville Rd	330-9330
Spice Station	1438 Blvd of the Arts	343-2894
State St Eating House	1533 State St	951-1533
Station 400	400 Lemon Ave	906-1400
Tamiami Tap	711 S Osprey Ave	500-3182
Turmeric	1001 Cocoanut Ave	212-2622
Yume Sushi	1532 Main St	363-0604

GULF GATE

Brine Seafood	2250 Gulf Gate Dr	404-5639
Dolce Italia	6606 Superior Ave	921-7007
Food + Beer	6528 Superior Ave	952-3361
Kiyoski's Sushi	6550 Gateway Ave	924-3781
Lovely Square	6559 Gateway Ave	724-2512
Monk's Steamer Bar	6690 Superior Ave	927-3388
Munchies 420 Café	6639 Superior Ave	929-9893
Opus Restaurant	6644 Gateway Ave	925-2313
Piccolo Italian Market	6518 Gateway Ave	923-2202
RomanSQ Pizza	6670 Superior Ave	237-8742
Schnitzel Kitchen	6521 Superior Ave	922-9299
Screaming Goat Taq.	6606 Superior Ave	210-3992

GULF GATE

Restaurant Name	Address	Phone #
Tony's Chicago Beef	6569 Superior Ave	922-7979
Veg	2164 Gulf Gate Dr	312-6424
Word of Mouth	6604 Gateway Ave	925-2400

LONGBOAT KEY & LIDO KEY

Drift Kitchen	700 Benjamin Franklin	388-2161
Dry Dock Waterfront	412 Gulf of Mexico Dr	383-0102
Euphemia Haye	5540 Gulf of Mexico Dr	383-3633
Lazy Lobster	5350 Gulf of Mexico Dr	388-0440
Harry's Continental Kit.	525 St Judes Dr	383-0777
Maison Blanche	2605 Gulf of Mexico Dr	383-8088
Mar-Vista Restaurant	760 Broadway St	383-2391
New Pass Grill	1505 Ken Thompson	388-3050

LAKEWOOD RANCH & UNIVERSITY PARK

Apollonia Grill	8235 Cooper Creek	359-4816
Dim Sum King	8194 Tourist Center Dr	306-5848
GROVE Restaurant	10670 Boardwalk Lp	893-4321
Inkawasi Peruvian	10667 Boardwalk Lp	360-1110
Jpan Sushi & Grill	229 N Cattlemen Rd	954-5726
Jersey Girl Bagels	5275 University Pkwy	388-8910
Mademoiselle Paris	8527 Cooper Creek Bl	355-2323
Nancy's Bar-B-Que	14475 SR 70	999-2390
Oak & Stone	5405 University Pkwy	225-4590
Tandoor	8453 Cooper Creek	926-3070

NORTH TAMIAMI TRAIL

Restaurant Name	Address	Phone #
Fork & Hen	2801 N Tamiami Trl	960-1212
Hob Nob Drive-In	1701 Washington Blvd	955-5001
Toasted Mango Café	430 N Tamiami Trl	388-7728
Wicked Cantina	1603 N Tamiami Trl	821-2990

ST. ARMANDS KEY

Blu Kouzina	25 N Blvd of Pres	388-2619
Café L'Europe	431 St Armands Cir	388-4415
Cha Cha Coconuts	417 St Armands Cir	388-3300
The Columbia	411 St Armands Cir	388-3987
Crab & Fin	420 St Armands Cir	388-3964
Lobstercraft	28 S Blvd of Pres	346-6325
Madison Avenue Deli	28 N Blvd of Pres	388-3354
St. Armands Oyster Bar	15 S Blvd of Pres	388-1334
Shore Diner	465 John Ringling Blvd	296-0303
Speaks Clam Bar	29 N Blvd of Pres	232-7633
Tommy Bahama Cafe	300 John Ringling Blvd	388-2888
Venizia	373 St Armands Cir	388-1400
Vernona	40 S Blvd of Pres	254-5877

SIESTA KEY

Anna's Deli	6535 Midnight Pass	348-4888
Big Water Fish Market	6641 Midnight Pass	554-8101
Bonjour French Cafe	5214 Ocean Blvd	346-0600
Café Gabbiano	5104 Ocean Blvd	349-1423

SIESTA KEY		
Restaurant Name	**Address**	**Phone #**
Capt. Curt's Oyster Bar	1200 Old Stickney Pt	349-3885
Clayton's Siesta Grille	1256 Old Stickney Pt	349-2800
The Cottage	153 Avenida Messina	312-9300
Daiquiri Deck Raw Bar	5250 Ocean Blvd	349-8697
Flavio's Siesta Key	5239 Ocean Blvd	349-0995
Gilligan's Island Bar	5253 Ocean Blvd	349-4759
The Hub Baha Grill	5148 Ocean Blvd	349-6800
Il Panificio	215 Avenida Madera	800-5570
Island House Tap & Grl.	5110 Ocean Blvd	312-9205
The Lobster Pot	5157 Ocean Blvd	349-2323
Miguel's	6631 Midnight Pass	349-4024
The Old Salty Dog	5023 Ocean Blvd	349-0158
Ophelia's on the Bay	9105 Midnight Pass	349-2212
Ripfire Pizza & BBQ	5218 Ocean Blvd	313-7511
Siesta Key Oyster Bar	5238 Ocean Blvd	346-5443
Spearfish Grille	1265 Old Stickney Pt	349-1970
Star Thai & Sushi	240 Avenida Madera	217-6758
The Summer House	149 Avenida Messina	206-2675
Sun Garden Café	210 Avenida Madera	346-7170
Toasted Mango Café	6621 Midnight Pass	552-6485
Turtle's	8875 Midnight Pass	346-2207
Village Café	5133 Ocean Blvd	349-2822

SOUTH TAMIAMI TRAIL		
Almazonica Cerveceria	4141 S Tamiami Trl	260-5964
Gecko's Grill & Pub	4870 S Tamiami Trl	923-8896

SOUTH TAMIAMI TRAIL		
Restaurant Name	Address	Phone #
Alpine Steakhouse	4520 S Tamiami Trl	922-3797
Connors Steakhouse	3501 S Tamiami Trl	260-3232
DaRuMa Japanese	4910 S. Tamiami Trl	552-9465
Demetrio's Pizzeria	4410 S Tamiami Trl	922-1585
Dutch Valley Rest.	6731 S Tamiami Trl	924-1770
Gentile Cheesesteaks	7523 S Tamiami Trl	926-0441
The Grasshopper	7253 S Tamiami Trl	923-3688
Marcello's Ristorante	4155 S Tamiami Trl	921-6794
Mattison's Forty One	7275 S Tamiami Trl	921-3400
Michael's On East	1212 East Ave	366-0007
Napule Ristorante	7129 S Tamiami Trl	556-9639
Phillippi Creek Oyster	5363 S Tamiami Trl	925-4444
Roessler's	2033 Vamo Way	966-5688
Sardinia	5770 S Tamiami Trl	702-8582
Stiks	4413 S Tamiami Trl	923-2742
Simon's Coffee House	5900 S Tamiami Trl	926-7151
Tripletail Seafood	4870 S Tamiami Trl	529-0555
Walt's Fish Market	4144 S Tamiami Trl	921-4605
Yummy House	1737 S Tamiami Trl	351-1688

SOUTHSIDE VILLAGE		
A Sprig of Thyme	1962 Hillview St	330-8890
Figaro Bistro	1944 Hillview St	960-2109
Ka Papa Cuisine	1830 S Osprey Ave	600-8590
Knick's Tavern & Grill	1818 S Osprey Ave	955-7761
Libby's Brasserie	1917 S Osprey Ave	487-7300

SOUTHSIDE VILLAGE

Restaurant Name	Address	Phone #
Meliora	1920 Hillview St	444-7692
Origin Beer & Pizza	3837 Hillview St	316-9222
Pacific Rim	1859 Hillview St	330-8071
Pazzo Southside	1830 S Osprey Ave	260-8831
Reef Cakes	1812 S Osprey Ave	444-7968
Southside Deli	1825 Hillview St	330-9302
Veronica Fish & Oyster	1830 S Osprey Ave	366-1342

SOUTHGATE

Andrea's	2085 Siesta Dr	951-9200
Baker & Wife	2157 Siesta Dr	960-1765
Connors Steakhouse	3501 S Tamiami Trl	260-3232
Fleming's Steakhouse	2001 Siesta Dr	358-9463
Rick's French Bistro	2177 Siesta Dr	957-0533

UNIVERSITY TOWN CENTER (UTC)

Brio Tuscan Grille	190 Univ Town Ctr Dr	702-9102
Burger & Beer Joint	160 Univ Town Ctr Dr	702-9915
The Capital Grille	180 Univ Town Ctr Dr	256-3647
Cheesecake Factory	130 Univ Town Ctr Dr	256-3760
Kona Grill	150 Univ Town Ctr Dr	256-8005
Rise Pies Pizza	140 Univ Town Ctr Dr	702-9920
Seasons 52	170 Univ Town Ctr Dr	702-9652
Sophies	120 Univ Town Ctr Dr	444-3077

LIVE MUSIC		
Restaurant Name	**Address**	**Phone #**
Capt. Curt's Oyster Bar	1200 Old Stickney Pt	349-3885
Casey Key Fish House	801 Blackburn Pt Rd	966-1901
Gecko's Grill & Pub	4870 S Tamiami Trl	923-8896
Gilligan's Island Bar	5253 Ocean Blvd	349-4759
The Hub Baha Grill	5148 Ocean Blvd	349-6800
JR's Old Packinghouse	987 S Packinghouse	371-9358
Marina Jack's	2 Marina Plaza	365-4243
Mattison's City Grille	1 N Lemon Ave	330-0440
Mattison's Forty One	7275 S Tamiami Trl	921-3400
Nancy's Bar-B-Que	14475 SR 70	999-2390
Nicky's On Palm	49 S Palm Ave	330-1727
O'Leary's Tiki Bar	5 Bayfront Dr	953-7505
Parrot Patio Bar & Grill	3602 Webber St	952-3352
Pop's Sunset Grill	112 Circuit Rd	488-3177
Sharky's on the Pier	1600 Harbor Dr S	488-1456
Siesta Key Oyster Bar	5238 Ocean Blvd	346-5443
Star Thai & Sushi	240 Avenida Madera	217-6758
Stottlemeyer's Smokehs	19 East Rd	312-5969
Tamiami Tap	711 S Osprey Ave	500-3182
Walt's Fish Market	4144 S Tamiami Trl	921-4605
CATERING		
Brick's Smoked Meats	1528 State St	993-1435
Daiquiri Deck Raw Bar	5250 Ocean Blvd	349-8697
Gecko's Grill & Pub	4870 S Tamiami Trl	923-8896
Harry's Continental Kit.	525 St Judes Dr	383-0777
JR's Old Packinghouse	987 S Packinghouse	371-9358

CATERING		
Restaurant Name	**Address**	**Phone #**
Mattison's Forty One	7275 S Tamiami Trl	921-3400
Michael's On East	1212 East Ave	366-0007
Nancy's Bar-B-Que	301 S Pineapple Ave	366-2271
Nellie's Deli	15 S Beneva Rd	924-2705
Village Café	5133 Ocean Blvd	349-2822
Zildjian Catering	6986 S Beneva Rd.	363-1709

EASY ON YOUR WALLET		
Athen's Family Rest.	2300 Bee Ridge Rd	706-4121
Anna's Deli	6535 Midnight Pass	348-4888
Baby Brie's Cafe	1938 Adams Ln	362-0988
The Breakfast House	1817 Fruitville Rd	366-6860
Brooklyn Bagels & Deli	6970 S Beneva Rd	993-1577
Casey Key Fish House	801 Blackburn Pt Rd	966-1901
Circo	1435 2nd St	253-0978
Dim Sum King	8194 Tourist Center Dr	306-5848
Doggystyle	1544 Main St	260-5835
Dutch Valley Rest.	6731 S Tamiami Trl	924-1770
El Toro Bravo	2720 Stickney Pt	924-0006
Faicco's Italian Hero's	3590 Webber St	960-1395
Gentile Cheesesteaks	7523 S Tamiami Trl	926-0441
Hob Nob Drive-In	1701 Washington Blvd	955-5001
Il Panificio	1703 Main St	366-5570
Island House Taqueria	2773 Bee Ridge Rd	922-8226
Jersey Girl Bagels	5275 University Pkwy	388-8910
Joey D's Chicago Style	3811 Kenny Dr.	378-8900

EASY ON YOUR WALLET		
Restaurant Name	**Address**	**Phone #**
Little Saigon Bistro	2725 S Beneva Rd	312-4730
Lovely Square	6559 Gateway Ave	724-2512
Main Bar Sandwich Shp	1944 Main St	955-8733
Michelle's Brown Bag	1819 Main St	365-5858
Munchies 420 Café	6639 Superior Ave	929-9893
New Pass Grill	1505 Ken Thompson	388-3050
Pastry Art Bakery	1512 Main St	955-7545
Pho Cali	1578 Main St	955-2683
Piccolo Italian Market	6518 Gateway Ave	923-2202
Reyna's Taqueria	935 N Beneva Rd	260-8343
Screaming Goat Taq.	6606 Superior Ave	210-3992
Simon's Coffee House	5900 S Tamiami Trl	926-7151
Stiks	4413 S Tamiami Trl	923-2742
Southside Deli	1825 Hillview St	330-9302
Sunnyside Cafe	4900 N Tamiami Trl	359-9500
Tony's Chicago Beef	6569 Superior Ave	922-7979
Yoder's Restaurant	3434 Bahia Vista	955-7771
Yokoso Ramen	3422 Clark Rd	265-1600
Wicked Cantina	1603 N Tamiami Trl	821-2990
BREAKFAST & LUNCH		
Anna's Deli	6535 Midnight Pass	348-4888
Baby Brie's Cafe	1938 Adams Ln	362-0988
BLVD Cafe	1580 Blvd of the Arts	203-8102
Bonjour French Cafe	5214 Ocean Blvd	346-0600
The Breakfast Company	7246 55th Ave E	201-6002

BREAKFAST & LUNCH		
Restaurant Name	**Address**	**Phone #**
The Breakfast House	1817 Fruitville Rd	366-6860
Brooklyn Bagels & Deli	6970 S Beneva Rd	993-1577
Lovely Square	6559 Gateway Ave	724-2512
Main Bar Sandwich Shp	1944 Main St	955-8733
Michelle's Brown Bag	1819 Main St	365-5858
Millie's Cafe	3900 Clark Rd	923-4054
Oasis Cafe	3542 S Osprey Ave	957-1214
Pastry Art Bakery	1512 Main St	955-7545
The Rosemary	411 N Orange Ave	955-7600
Simon's Coffee House	5900 S Tamiami Trl	926-7151
Southside Deli	1825 Hillview St	330-9302
Station 400	400 Lemon Ave	906-1400
Sun Garden Café	210 Avenida Madera	346-7170
Tahini Beach Cafe	103 Gulf Dr N	251-4022
Toasted Mango Café	6621 Midnight Pass	552-6485
Village Café	5133 Ocean Blvd	349-2822
Word of Mouth	6604 Gateway Ave	925-2400
NEW		
Baby Brie's Cafe	1938 Adams Ln	362-0988
Blue Koi	3801 McIntosh Rd	388-7738
BLVD Cafe	1580 Blvd of the Arts	203-8102
The Breakfast Company	7246 55th Ave E	201-6002
Chateau 13	535 13th St W	226-0110
Faicco's Italian Hero's	3590 Webber St	960-1395
Flirt Sushi Lounge	1296 1st St	342-2122
Good Liquid Brewing Co	1570 Lakefront Dr	238-6466

NEW		
Restaurant Name	**Address**	**Phone #**
Grandpa's Schnitzel	2700 Stickney Pt Rd	922-3888
Graze Street AMI	3218 E Bay- Holmes B	896-6320
Kore Steakhouse	1561 Lakefront Dr	928-5673
LobsterCraft	28A S Blvd of Pres	346-6325
Meliora	1920 Hillview St	444-7692
Molly's Resaurant & Pub	1562 Main St	366-7711
Opus Restaurant	6644 Gateway Ave	925-2313
St. Armands Oyster Bar	15 S Blvd of Pres	388-1334
Tahini Brach Cafe	103 Gulf Dr N -BtnBh	251-4022
Turmeric	1001 Cocoanut Ave	212-2622
Yokoso Ramen	3422 Clark Rd	265-1600

SUSHI		
Blue Koi	3801 Macintosh Rd	388-7738
DaRuMa Japanese	5459 Fruitville Rd	342-6600
DaRuMa Japanese	4910 S. Tamiami Trl	552-9465
Drunken Poet Café	1572 Main St	955-8404
Flirt Sushi Lounge	1296 1st St	342-2122
Jpan Sushi & Grill	3 Paradise Plaza	954-5726
Jpan Sushi & Grill	229 N Cattlemen Rd	954-5726
Kiyoski's Sushi	6550 Gateway Ave	924-3781
Kojo	1289 N Palm Ave	536-9717
Pacific Rim	1859 Hillview St	330-8071
Spice Station	1438 Blvd of the Arts	343-2894
Star Thai & Sushi	240 Avenida Madera	217-6758
Yume Sushi	1532 Main St	363-0604

SPORTS + FOOD + FUN

Restaurant Name	Address	Phone #
Capt. Curt's Oyster Bar	1200 Old Stickney Pt	349-3885
Daiquiri Deck Raw Bar	5250 Ocean Blvd	349-8697
Gecko's Grill & Pub	6606 S Tamiami Trl	248-2020
Gecko's Grill & Pub	1900 Hillview St	953-2929
Gecko's Grill & Pub	5588 Palmer Crossing	923-6061
Oak & Stone	5405 University Pkwy	225-4590
The Old Salty Dog	5023 Ocean Blvd	349-0158
Parrot Patio Bar & Grill	3602 Webber St	952-3352
Patrick's 1481	1481 Main St	955-1481
Siesta Key Oyster Bar	5238 Ocean Blvd	346-5443

GREAT BURGERS

Alpine Steakhouse	4520 S Tamiami Trl	922-3797
BrewBurgers Pub	360 Commercial Ct	484-2337
Cha Cha Coconuts	417 St Armands Cir	388-3300
Connors Steakhouse	3501 S. Tamiami Trl	260-3232
Daiquiri Deck Raw Bar	5250 Ocean Blvd	349-8697
Daiquiri Deck Raw Bar	325 John Ringling Blvd	388-3325
Daiquiri Deck Raw Bar	300 W Venice Ave	488-0649
Daiquiri Deck Raw Bar	1250 Stickney Pt Rd	312-2422
Gecko's Grill & Pub	4870 S Tamiami Trl	923-8896
Gecko's Grill & Pub	1900 Hillview St	953-2929
Gecko's Grill & Pub	5588 Palmer Crossing	923-6061
Gecko's Grill & Pub	351 N Cattlemen Rd	378-0077

GREAT BURGERS

Restaurant Name	Address	Phone #
Food + Beer	6528 Superior Ave	952-3361
Hob Nob Drive-In	1701 Washington Blvd	955-5001
Indigenous	239 Links Ave	706-4740
Island House Tap & Grl.	5110 Ocean Blvd	312-9205
JR's Old Packinghouse	987 S Packinghouse	371-9358
Knick's Tavern & Grill	1818 S Osprey Ave	955-7761
Libby's Brasserie	1917 S Osprey Ave	487-7300
Made	1990 Main St	953-2900
Munchies 420 Café	6639 Superior Ave	929-9893
New Pass Grill	1505 Ken Thompson	388-3050
Parrot Patio Bar & Grill	3602 Webber St	952-3352
Patrick's 1481	1481 Main St	955-1481
Pop's Sunset Grill	112 Circuit Rd	488-3177
The Public House	6240 N Lockwood Rg	822-0795
Shakespeare's	3550 S Osprey Ave	364-5938
Sharky's on the Pier	1600 Harbor Dr S	488-1456
Tony's Chicago Beef	6569 Superior Ave	922-7979
Village Café	5133 Ocean Blvd	349-2822

NICE WINE LIST

Amore	180 N Lime Ave	383-1111
Andrea's	2085 Siesta Dr	951-9200
Baker & Wife	2157 Siesta Dr	960-1765
Beach Bistro	6600 Gulf Dr N	778-6444

NICE WINE LIST		
Restaurant Name	Address	Phone #
Bevardi's Salute!	23 N Lemon Ave	365-1020
Bijou Café	1287 First St	366-8111
Café Barbosso	5501 Palmer Crossing	922-7999
Café Gabbiano	5104 Ocean Blvd	349-1423
Café L'Europe	431 St Armands Cir	388-4415
Connors Steakhouse	3501 S Tamiami Trl	260-3232
Dolce Italia	6606 Superior Ave	921-7007
Duval's, Fresh, Local...	1435 Main St	312-4001
Euphemia Haye	5540 Gulf of Mexico Dr	383-3633
Figaro Bistro	1944 Hillview St	960-2109
Fins At Sharky's	1600 Harbor Dr S	999-3467
Flavio's Siesta Key	5239 Ocean Blvd	349-0995
GROVE Restaurant	10670 Boardwalk Lp	893-4321
Harry's Continental Kit.	525 St Judes Dr	383-0777
Indigenous	239 Links Ave	706-4740
Jack Dusty	1111 Ritz-Carlton Dr	309-2266
Maison Blanche	2605 Gulf of Mexico Dr	383-8088
Mattison's Forty One	7275 S Tamiami Trl	921-3400
Melange	1568 Main St	953-7111
Michael John's	1040 Carlton Arms	747-8032
Michael's On East	1212 East Ave	366-0007
Miguel's	6631 Midnight Pass	349-4024
Napule Ristorante	7129 S Tamiami Trl	556-9639

NICE WINE LIST		
Restaurant Name	Address	Phone #
Ophelia's on the Bay	9105 Midnight Pass	349-2212
Pier 22	1200 1st Avenue W	748-8087
Roessler's	2033 Vamo Way	966-5688
Rosebud's Steakhouse	2215 S Tamiami Trl	918-8771
Rosemary & Thyme	511 N Orange Ave	955-7600
Sage	1216 1st St	445-5660
Sardinia	5770 S Tamiami Trl	702-8582
State St Eating House	1533 State St	951-1533
The Summer House	149 Avenida Messina	206-2675
Selva Grill	1345 Main St	362-4427
Veronica Fish & Oyster	1830 S Osprey Ave	366-1342

HELP MAKE A DIFFERENCE IN OUR SARASOTA-MANATEE COMMUNITY

Listed below are two local organizations that are striving to assist those in need in our Sarasota area. They could use your help. Please consider a donation to either (or both) during 2023.

ALL FAITHS FOOD BANK
WHAT THEY NEED: Donations of non-perishable, frozen, and perishable food items needed. Monetary donations are also accepted and can be made directly through their website.
MORE INFO: allfaithsfoodbank.org

MAYOR'S FEED THE HUNGRY PROGRAM
WHAT THEY NEED: Donations of food, time, and money are needed. This program hosts a large food drive in the month of November. Check their website for details or to make a monetary donation.
MORE INFO: mayorsfeedthehungry.org

A BEAUTIFUL WATER VIEW		
Restaurant Name	Address	Phone #
Beach Bistro	6600 Gulf Dr N	778-6444
Casey Key Fish House	801 Blackburn Pt Rd	966-1901
The Crow's Nest	1968 Tarpon Ctr Dr	484-9551
Drift Kitchen	700 Benjamin Franklin	388-2161
Dry Dock Waterfront	412 Gulf of Mexico Dr	383-0102
Fins At Sharky's	1600 Harbor Dr S	999-3467
Jack Dusty	1111 Ritz-Carlton Dr	309-2266
Mar-Vista Restaurant	760 Broadway St	383-2391
Marina Jack's	2 Marina Plaza	365-4243
New Pass Grill	1505 Ken Thompson	388-3050
The Old Salty Dog	160 Ken Thompson Pk	388-4311
The Old Salty Dog	1485 S Tamiami Trl	483-1000
O'Leary's Tiki Bar	5 Bayfront Dr	953-7505
Ophelia's on the Bay	9105 Midnight Pass	349-2212
Phillippi Creek Oyster	5363 S Tamiami Trl	925-4444
Pier 22	1200 1st Avenue W	748-8087
Pop's Sunset Grill	112 Circuit Rd	488-3177
Sharky's on the Pier	1600 Harbor Dr S	488-1456
Turtle's	8875 Midnight Pass	346-2207

LATER NIGHT MENU		
Café Epicure	1298 Main St	366-5648
Capt. Curt's Oyster Bar	1200 Old Stickney Pt	349-3885
Casey Key Fish House	801 Blackburn Pt Rd	966-1901
Circo	1435 2nd St	253-0978

LATER NIGHT MENU		
Restaurant Name	**Address**	**Phone #**
The Cottage	153 Avenida Messina	312-9300
Daiquiri Deck Raw Bar	5250 Ocean Blvd	349-8697
Drunken Poet Café	1572 Main St	955-8404
El Melvin Cocina	1355 Main St	366-1618
Flavio's Siesta Key	5239 Ocean Blvd	349-0995
Food + Beer	6528 Superior Ave	952-3361
Gecko's Grill & Pub	6606 S Tamiami Trl	248-2020
Gecko's Grill & Pub	1900 Hillview St	953-2929
Gilligan's Island Bar	5253 Ocean Blvd	349-4759
The Hub Baha Grill	5148 Ocean Blvd	349-6800
Island House Tap & Grl.	5110 Ocean Blvd	312-9205
JR's Old Packinghouse	987 S Packinghouse	371-9358
Made	1990 Main St	953-2900
Mattison's City Grille	1 N Lemon Ave	330-0440
Melange	1568 Main St	953-7111
Monk's Steamer Bar	6690 Superior Ave	927-3388
Munchies 420 Café	6639 Superior Ave	929-9893
Origin Beer & Pizza	3837 Hillview St	316-9222
Patrick's 1481	1481 Main St	955-1481
Sharky's on the Pier	1600 Harbor Dr S	488-1456
Siesta Key Oyster Bar	5238 Ocean Blvd	346-5443
Tamiami Tap	711 S Osprey Ave	500-3182
Walt's Fish Market	4144 S Tamiami Trl	921-4605

SARASOTA FINE & FINER DINING		
Restaurant Name	Address	Phone #
A Sprig of Thyme	1962 Hillview St	330-8890
Andrea's	2085 Siesta Dr	951-9200
Beach Bistro	6600 Gulf Dr N	778-6444
Bijou Café	1287 First St	366-8111
Café L'Europe	431 St Armands Cir	388-4415
The Crow's Nest	1968 Tarpon Ctr Dr	484-9551
Euphemia Haye	5540 Gulf of Mexico Dr	383-3633
Indigenous	239 Links Ave	706-4740
Jack Dusty	1111 Ritz-Carlton Dr	309-2266
Maison Blanche	2605 Gulf of Mexico Dr	383-8088
Melange	1568 Main St	953-7111
Michael's On East	1212 East Ave	366-0007
Ophelia's on the Bay	9105 Midnight Pass	349-2212
Pier 22	1200 1st Avenue W	748-8087
Sage	1216 1st St	445-5660
The Summer House	149 Avenida Messina	206-2675

PIZZA PIE!		
Atmosphere	935 N Beneva Rd	203-8542
Baker & Wife	2157 Siesta Dr	960-1765
Bavaro's Pizza	27 Fletcher Ave	552-9131
Café Barbosso	5501 Palmer Crossing	922-7999
Café Epicure	1298 Main St	366-5648
Caragiulos	69 S Palm Ave	951-0866

PIZZA PIE!		
Restaurant Name	**Address**	**Phone #**
1592 Wood Fired Kitch	1592 Main St	365-2234
Flavio's Siesta Key	5239 Ocean Blvd	349-0995
Il Panificio	1703 Main St	366-5570
Joey D's Chicago Style	3811 Kenny Dr.	378-8900
Mattison's City Grille	1 N Lemon Ave	330-0440
Mediterraneo	1970 Main St	365-4122
Napule Ristorante	7129 S Tamiami Trl	556-9639
Oak & Stone	5405 University Pkwy	225-4590
Origin Beer & Pizza	3837 Hillview St	316-9222
Pizza N' Brew	1507 Main St	359-3894
Ripfire Pizza & BBQ	5218 Ocean Blvd	313-7511
RomanSQ Pizza	6670 Superior Ave	237-8742
Venizia	373 St Armands Cir	388-1400

UPSCALE CHAIN DINING		
Bonefish Grill	3971 S Tamiami Trl	924-9090
Bravo Coastal Kitchen	3501 S Tamiami Trl	316-0868
Brio Tuscan Grille	190 Univ Town Ctr Dr	702-9102
California Pizza Kitchen	192 N Cattlemen Rd	203-6966
The Capital Grille	180 Univ Town Ctr Dr	256-3647
Fleming's Steakhouse	2001 Siesta Dr	358-9463
Kona Grill	150 Univ Town Ctr Dr	256-8005
P.F. Changs	766 S Osprey Ave	296-6002
Seasons 52	170 Univ Town Ctr Dr	702-9652

YOUR SARASOTA FOOD JOURNAL
RESTAURANT & TASTING NOTES

....

....

....

....

....

....

....

....

....

....

....

....

....

....

....

....

....